John Hadamuscin's
DOWN HOME

John Hadamuscin's
DOWN HOME

A Year of
Cooking,
Entertaining,
and Living Easy

Photographs
by
Randy O'Rourke

Harmony Books
New York

Also by John Hadamuscin

Simple Pleasures
101 THOUGHTS AND RECIPES
FOR SAVORING THE LITTLE THINGS IN LIFE

From My House to Yours
GIFTS, RECIPES, AND REMEMBRANCES
FROM THE HEARTH AND HOME

Enchanted Evenings
DINNERS, SUPPERS, PICNICS, AND PARTIES

Special Occasions
HOLIDAY ENTERTAINING ALL YEAR ROUND

The Holidays
ELEGANT ENTERTAINING
FROM THANKSGIVING TO TWELFTH NIGHT

Published by Harmony Books, a division of Crown Publishers, Inc.,
201 East 50th Street, New York, New York 10022.
Member of the Crown Publishing Group. Random House, Inc.
New York, Toronto, London, Sydney, Auckland

HARMONY and colophon are trademarks of Crown Publishers, Inc.

Manufactured in Japan

LIBRARY OF CONGRESS CATALOGING-IN-PUBLICATION DATA

Hadamuscin, John.
[Down Home]
John Hadamuscin's down home:
a year of cooking, entertaining, and living easy/
by John Hadamuscin—1st ed.
p. cm.
Includes index.
1. Cookery, American. 2. Country life—Ohio. I. Title.
TX715. H123 1993
641.5973—dc20 92-43579
CIP

ISBN 0-517-58931-1
10 9 8 7 6 5 4 3 2 1
First Edition

Designed by Ken Sansone

For
Mom, Dad,
Joe, Larry,
and Betty
— my family

Thanks

Once again, I've been fortunate enough to have the same wonderful people working with me who are always willing to share the long hours, the hard work, and the fun (and the food!). So, thanks to the members of the "crew," who always do the impossible, who help translate what's in my head onto the printed page—I couldn't do it without them:

Photographer Randy O'Rourke, as usual, turned in a great performance, and he continues to make me laugh with his corny jokes and songs. He's always willing to change a camera angle or a light or chase a sunset across a field to make a picture better. Thanks to Randy's wife, Stephanie, and son, Tiernan, who were frequently on hand and always willing to join in. Crown's creative director, Ken Sansone, is the best, first listening to my wild ideas and then making them work. Finally, a big hug to Clara Henry, my mom. She continues to amaze me— she has more energy than any of us. When she comes for a visit she jumps right in—if she's not helping to test recipes she's on the spot cooking for the pictures. Everyone should be lucky enough to have a such a mother. How grateful I am to have such a great crew!

There's a second crew—the Crown-Harmony publishing team, who take over when the first crew is done. Publisher Michelle Sidrane and Editor-in-Chief Betty A. Prashker have always supported my work and believed in this book from the start (and Michelle picked me some elderberries, too!). A hug to my new editor, Shaye Areheart, a "down-home girl" herself, my cheerleader and confidante. And thanks to the rest of the gang who make these books go: Joan Denman, Amy Boorstein, Laurie Stark, Peter Guzzardi, Jo Fagan, Phyllis Fleiss, Virginia Van Dyk, Barbara Marks, Hilary Bass, Wendy Schuman, Bruce Harris, Chip Gibson, Steve Magnuson, Joan DeMayo, Gail Shanks, Pam Romano, Kelly Hammond, and Linda Gelbard.

My agent, Diane Cleaver, really believed in *Down Home* and she always has an encouraging word when I need it. And again, thanks to Esther Mitgang, who first encouraged me to do a book and started this whole crazy thing that I love so much.

And there are the usual family and friends who continue along at my side. I'm lucky to have them. My family, Larry, Joyce, Heather, and Rob, traveled from Ohio to spend Thanksgiving and take part in the photo shoot. My father, John Hadamuscin, Sr., watched over his garden daily to make sure it was perfect for photography when we went home to Ohio. My friends Tom and Fran Barnes, John Coll, Ken Daniels, Nolan Drummond, Bob Gibbons, Hal Good, Bernita Goth, Joyce Gould, Rose Grant, Dana and Renie Landry, Iva Mae Montalbano, Bob Schuman, the Shepacks, Janet Sutherland, Pam Thomas, Cheryl Valentine, and my nieces Kimberly Mills and JoAnn Boyer all helped in one way or another as they always do.

Finally, thanks to all of you, my extended family, many of whom I've met in my travels. I hope this book brings back some pleasant memories.

Contents

FALL

୧ନ

WINTER

୧ନ

Introduction

❧

It was a warm August day with a gentle breeze—just right for a Sunday ride in the country. A call to a few friends and we were off antiquing in eastern Pennsylvania. It was a wonderful day, full of laughs, a good lunch, and even a few good buys. We headed back toward the city in the early afternoon and, wanting to prolong the day, we ventured across unknown back roads of New Jersey, past horse farms, through woodlands and marshlands, not looking at a map, but heading in a somewhat easterly direction.

About twenty-five miles outside the city, we suddenly passed a red farmhouse with a FOR SALE sign out front. I turned the car around, drove past the house again, took the number, called the realtor, and was shown the house. The next weekend I looked at the house again, and then spent the rest of the day touring the area. During the next few weeks I looked at many other houses in the area, "just to be sure," but I always returned to the red farmhouse. The house remained in my thoughts, and of course I was already thinking about what it would be like if it were mine.

The owners were visiting their native England and I had to wait six anxious weeks until they returned. Finally, I met them at the house. They were a delightful couple who proudly gave me the full tour, pointing out all those little details a realtor could never know: the potting shed under the back porch, the rock foundation out back where the chicken house once stood, the site of the barn where a neighbor's house now stands. As we walked around the grounds, along stone walls and under century-old black walnut and oak trees and ancient overgrown lilac bushes, I was consumed by the smell of fresh-cut grass and blooming roses. Suddenly I was in another place and another time, back at the Ohio farmhouse where I grew up. I knew then for sure that this was "home."

I suppose it was inevitable that I come back to the country full-time. After years of racing to the country on Friday afternoons, then racing back to the city when the weekend was over, I gradually started making the weekends longer, and began to really savor the peace and quiet the country offered, the hours spent digging around in the dirt of the garden and puttering around the kitchen made me feel good. But I really hadn't given any serious thought to moving out of the city for good. I suppose it was just fate—at heart, I'm really still a country boy.

So, I've come home again. Not really back home, but it's almost the country and ever so slightly closer to Ohio and the farmhome of my childhood. I've got a big kitchen with plenty of room to spread out and an office where I can close the door and leave work behind and a garden I can dig in any day at all. And out here I've got all the things small-town living has to offer (but I'm less than an hour from the city and can have all it offers as well). Most important, though, is that I live in a place that really feels like home.

I've been here almost two years now, and I often wonder about the people who knew this house before I did, the babies who were born here, the young men who went off to war from here, the brides who took that momentous step from the front door. What stories these people could tell, some sad, others joyous and lively. I remind myself that "our" house has survived storms and blizzards outside, tragedies and disappointments inside. As Edgar Guest said, "it takes a heap of living to make a house a home."

This home I call mine is a place I love. I truly believe houses respond to people and that this 130-year-old house, as it has done with its past visitors, has taken me in and accepted me and likes me right back. As I have adapted to the house, it has adapted to me, too. When I'm weary and need to be alone, it is quiet, and when I want to have a houseful of guests over a weekend, it is always ready to welcome them in, just as our big Victorian farmhouse did when I was growing up. This house has helped me have a clearer view of how and why I like to have people in and it has helped us all share good food and good times together.

When I plan get-togethers these days, I certainly don't hold a barn raising, like country folks used to do, but I have found myself planning such diverse events as a simple meat loaf supper for a few neighbors on a snowy Sunday night and an ice cream social for a crowd of family and friends on the Fourth of July. I've come back around to the days when having company didn't mean putting on the dog but only meant adding another side dish or two to the every day table. Out with all the fancy high-falutin' multicourse dinner parties and back to the simplicity of "come on over for coffee and cake."

Lately I've realized that no matter how "sophisticated" or how much of a "city slicker" I may have thought I'd become, much of my taste and most of my habits reflect my rural Midwestern background. No matter what kinds of complex cooking methods, exotic ingredients, or unorthodox combinations I may experiment with, I always find myself returning to the simple ways and simple foods of our Ohio farmhouse kitchen. I'm not saying that I've thrown away every influence that's changed me since I left home for the big city; I often do use a lot of the old ingredients and methods in new ways. But I don't want to slave away in the kitchen trying to single-handedly duplicate the efforts of the moment's hot restaurant chef and his staff. And if you're like me, you don't entertain to impress in the first place. Your family and friends will love you just the same whether you serve them a fancy hours-in-the-kitchen show-off dessert or a slice of old-fashioned chocolate cake (in fact, I'll bet they'll love you a little more just for baking the cake in the first place).

So here is a yearful of my new "special occasions" at home, celebrating everything from the first warm evening in spring to Christmas day. These are times that my family, friends, and I have enjoyed together at my house, and I hope they help make some good times at your house, too.

John Hadamuscin
Walnut Hill, 1993

Pancakes for Breakfast

Basic Buttermilk Pancakes

Whole Wheat–Fruit Pancakes

Gingerbread Pancakes

Corn Cakes

Chocolate Chip–Banana
Pancakes

Cottage Cheese Pancakes

Oatmeal Pancakes

Buckwheat Pancakes

Blueberry Buckwheat Pancakes

. . .

Blueberry Syrup

Strawberry Syrup

Pineapple Syrup

Ginger Pear Honey

Apples in Brown Sugar Sauce

Cinnamon Yogurt and Fruit

Sweet Ricotta and Berries

Lemon Syrup

Flavored Butters, Maple Syrups,
and Fruit Syrups

Pancake breakfasts are a Midwest tradition. They began as annual events where folks would get together at the grange hall or church hall for food and fellowship. Over the years, the breakfasts have evolved into fund-raisers for various local causes, from the fire department to a local relief fund. When I came to Chatham, I was happy to see that, here too, a pancake breakfast is an annual springtime event. There's no better season for pancakes than springtime, when the sap of the sugar maple is running and fresh syr-up is made.

I, of course, have long been a pancake lover. When we were kids, my brothers and I would

**The pancake man (above)
announces the annual breakfast at
the middle school here in Chatham.**

**Stacks of buttermilk pancakes
hot off the griddle (opposite).**

have pancake-eating contests, and our little sister would keep up with us for at least the first two or three. But Mom, commandeering the griddle, could barely make the pancakes fast enough to keep up with three hungry boys.

The pancake breakfasts of my childhood consisted of buttermilk pancakes slathered with our own sweet butter and maple syrup made by our neighbors, the Bauers. Since then I've experimented with a variety of pancakes and all kinds of toppings; here are some of my favorites.

Getting Ready I'm not suggesting that anyone make all these pancakes at once, but if you're having a crowd, it might be fun to have two different batters at the ready, along with an electric griddle to help expand the stove top. Even if you're having only one kind of pancake, it's a good idea to have two or three toppings available.

The batter for the Oatmeal Pancakes needs to be made a few hours in advance, so the night before is probably most convenient. Any of the other batters can be made just before breakfast time, because each only takes a few minutes (pancake batters can be made a day in advance and refrigerated, too). Have any toppings ready before you start cooking the pancakes (everything except sliced fresh fruit can be made a day in advance), and make sure a pitcher of chilled juice and a pot of hot coffee is ready.

Basic Buttermilk Pancakes

MAKES ABOUT 1 DOZEN

This basic recipe can be varied endlessly. Follow the suggestions below or make your own additions.

1¼ cups all-purpose flour
2 tablespoons sugar
½ teaspoon salt
1 teaspoon baking powder
½ teaspoon baking soda
2 large eggs
1 cup buttermilk
2 tablespoons vegetable oil or melted
    butter
Vegetable shortening

1. In a batter bowl (or medium mixing bowl), sift together the flour, sugar, salt, baking powder, and baking soda. In a separate small bowl, beat the eggs, buttermilk, and oil together, then add to the dry mixture, mixing until the dry ingredients are just moistened. It's okay if the batter is slighty lumpy.

2. In a large, heavy skillet or on a griddle over medium heat, heat enough shortening to just cover the bottom of the skillet. Once it is sizzling, pour or spoon the batter, about ¼ cup per pancake, into the skillet. When small bubbles appear on the surface and the edges begin to brown, turn them and cook until lightly browned on the other side.

3. Transfer the pancakes to a platter and keep warm while cooking the remaining pancakes.

Whole Wheat–Fruit Pancakes Substitute 1 cup whole wheat flour for 1 cup all-purpose flour and add 1 thinly sliced banana, 1 cup blueberries, or 1 cup chopped peaches.

Gingerbread Pancakes Substitute 3 tablespoons molasses for the sugar and add 2 teaspoons ground ginger and 2 teaspoons ground cinnamon with the other dry ingredients. Add ⅔ cup diced apple or pears if you'd like.

Corn Cakes Substitute ¾ cup cornmeal for ¾ cup of the flour and add 1 cup cooked corn.

Chocolate Chip–Banana Pancakes Add ½ teaspoon ground cinnamon to the dry ingredients and stir ⅔ cup semisweet chocolate chips and 1 thinly sliced banana into the batter.

Cottage Cheese Pancakes

MAKES 8 TO 10

Serve these with applesauce, Ginger Pear Honey (page 16), or Apples in Brown Sugar Sauce (page 16).

1 cup small curd lowfat cottage cheese
3 large eggs, lightly beaten
¼ cup flour
2 tablespoons butter, melted
1 tablespoon sugar
½ teaspoon ground cinnamon
¼ teaspoon salt
Vegetable shortening

1. Line a strainer with a double layer of cheesecloth. Place the cottage cheese in the strainer and press the cottage cheese lightly with the back of a spoon to drain off the liquid.

2. In a mixing bowl, beat the eggs lightly with a fork. Add the cottage cheese and the remaining ingredients except the shortening and beat until just blended.

3. In a large, heavy skillet or on a griddle over medium heat, heat enough shortening to just cover the bottom of the skillet. Once it is sizzling, drop the batter by tablespoonfuls into the skillet. When the pancakes are brown at the edges, turn them and continue cooking until lightly browned on the other side, 2 to 3 minutes longer.

4. Transfer the pancakes to a platter and keep warm while cooking the remaining pancakes.

Cottage Cheese Pancakes with Cinnamon Yogurt (page 17) and sliced strawberries.

PANCAKE-MAKING TIPS

• When making pancake batters, mix them just until the dry ingredients are moistened. It's okay to leave the batter a little lumpy; the lumps will disappear as the pancakes cook.

• If you have a batter bowl with a spouted lip, use it for making pancake batter; pouring batter onto the griddle is easier than spooning it on. (A batter bowl, available at any housewares store, is a good investment; use it for making cakes or mixing anything pourable.)

• Grease the skillet or griddle lightly. A nonstick griddle is best of all, since it needs no greasing. The fat in the batter will help keep the pancakes from sticking.

• To test the heat of the griddle or skillet, splash a few drops of cold water onto it. If the water dances and sizzles, the skillet is ready. For most

pancakes, set the temperature of an electric skillet or griddle at 350° F.

• Use no more than ¼ cup of batter for each pancake so the pancakes are manageable and easy to turn.

• Once the edges of the pancake are lightly browned and the surface starts to bubble, the pancake is ready to be turned. The second side will take a little less time to cook than the first.

• Keep pancakes warm while you're making the rest by arranging them in a single layer on an ovenproof platter or a baking sheet and placing them in a slow oven.

• Leftover pancakes (who ever heard of such a thing?!) can be frozen individually, then stacked and packed into plastic bags for freezer storage. Reheat frozen pancakes in a single layer on a baking sheet in a moderate oven.

Oatmeal Pancakes

MAKES ABOUT 1 DOZEN

¾ cup quick-cooking oats
1 cup buttermilk
2 tablespoons molasses
2 large eggs
2 tablespoons vegetable oil
½ cup all-purpose flour
1½ teaspoons baking soda
½ teaspoon salt
½ teaspoon ground cinnamon
Vegetable shortening

1. In a small bowl, combine the oats, buttermilk, and molasses. Cover and refrigerate overnight (or at least 2 hours).

2. Add the eggs and oil to the oat mixture and mix well. Add the flour, baking soda, salt, and cinnamon and mix well.

3. In a large, heavy skillet or on a griddle over medium heat, heat enough shortening to just cover the bottom of the skillet. Once it is sizzling, pour the batter, about ¼ cup per pancake, into the skillet. When small bubbles appear on

the surface and the edges begin to brown, turn, and cook until lightly browned on the other side.

4. Transfer the pancakes to a platter and keep warm while cooking the remaining pancakes.

Variations Add any of the following: 1 thinly sliced ripe banana and ½ cup chopped pecans; ⅔ cup blueberries or sliced strawberries; or ½ cup raisins and ½ cup chopped walnuts.

Buckwheat Pancakes

MAKES ABOUT 1½ DOZEN

¾ cup wholewheat flour
½ cup buckwheat flour
1 tablespoon sugar
½ teaspoon salt
1 teaspoon baking powder
½ teaspoon baking soda
2 large eggs, separated
1 cup buttermilk
2 tablespoons vegetable oil or melted butter

1. In a batter bowl (or medium mixing bowl), sift together the flours, sugar, salt, baking pow-

der, and baking soda. In a separate small bowl, beat the egg yolks, buttermilk, and oil together, then add to the dry mixture, mixing until the dry ingredients are just moistened. It's okay if the batter is slightly lumpy.

2. In another bowl, beat the egg whites until stiff but not dry, then fold them into the batter.

3. In a large, heavy skillet or on a griddle over medium heat, heat enough shortening to just cover the bottom of the skillet until sizzling. Pour the batter, about ¼ cup per pancake, into the skillet. When small bubbles appear on the surface and the edges begin to brown, turn them and cook until lightly browned on the other side.

4. Transfer the pancakes to a platter and keep warm while cooking the remaining pancakes.

Blueberry Buckwheat Pancakes Add 1 cup blueberries to the batter.

Blueberry Syrup

MAKES ABOUT 2½ CUPS

1 pint blueberries
1 cup sugar
½ cup water

Combine all the ingredients in a small, heavy saucepan and stir to blend. Cook over low heat, stirring and pressing the berries against the side of the pan to crush them slightly, until the berries are softened and the mixture is syrupy, about 10 minutes. Serve warm or cool.

Strawberry Syrup Substitute 1 pint strawberries, hulled and sliced.

Pineapple Syrup Substitute 2 cups (one 20-ounce can) crushed pineapple for the berries and ½ cup firmly packed brown sugar for half the granulated sugar. Add a tablespoon or so of rum if you'd like.

Oatmeal Pancakes with Pink Applesauce (page 101) and raspberries (top), and Blueberry Buckwheat Pancakes with Blueberry Syrup and melting butter (right).

SUGARTIME

Maple sugaring is an annual ritual that begins at the first thaw of spring, when the sap of the sugar maple starts running. The sugaring is done by inserting a small trough into a small hole drilled into the side of the trunk of a tree, hanging a bucket from the trough, and waiting for the sap to drip into the bucket. To make syrup, buckets of sap are taken to sugarhouses in the midst of the sugar camps, where the sap is boiled down in big drums (it takes thirty-five to forty gallons of sap to make one gallon of syrup), sending big clouds of steam into the chilly early spring air. (The Indians, who first introduced the American settlers to the sweetening powers of the

maple, didn't stop the process of boiling the sap at the syrup stage, but went on to make maple sugar, for storage purposes. The maple sugar became popular among the settlers as a cheaper alternative to the expensive white sugar imported from the West Indies.

Of all the states, Ohio is the third-largest maple sugar producer, and one of my favorite childhood memories is of the times when we'd visit our neighbors, the Bauers, who had a sugar camp, during sugartime. We kids would all be given a little bit of fresh hot maple syrup to make a simple candy we called "maple snow" by pouring it onto the surface of pure, newly fallen snow. (In New England it's traditional to serve this taffylike confection with doughnuts, hot coffee, and sour pickle—the sour pickle is said to bring out the maple flavor!) And then we'd take home a tin of syrup, which of course required the making of pancakes!

Ginger Pear Honey

MAKES ABOUT 3 PINTS

This very old recipe produces a thick amber syrup, made by cooking down pears and apple juice, that looks and pours like honey. It's a delicious companion for pancakes, especially Cottage Cheese Pancakes and Gingerbread Pancakes. It's good with waffles and ice cream, too.

4 cups apple juice
2 cups water
Juice of 1 lemon
4 pounds tart, flavorful pears, quartered pared, and cored (do not peel)
6 cups sugar
Grated rind of 1 lemon
1 small cinnamon stick, crushed
1 tablespoon chopped gingerroot

1. Combine the apple juice, water, and lemon juice in a large, nonreactive saucepan. Coarsely grate the apples and add them immediately to the pan. Place the pan over medium-high heat and bring the mixture to a boil. Gradually stir in the sugar, stirring until it dissolves. Add the lemon rind, cinnamon stick, and gingerroot.

2. Reduce the heat to low and simmer, uncovered, until the liquid is thick and syrupy, about 1 hour. The cooled mixture should be the consistency of honey; test by dropping a spoonful onto a small plate and chilling briefly.

3. Strain the mixture, then ladle it into half-pint jars or 1-pint bottles, leaving ¼ inch of space at the top. Seal and process in a boiling water bath for 15 minutes, cool, and store in a cool place.

Apples in Brown Sugar Sauce

MAKES ABOUT 4 CUPS

Delicious with Whole Wheat–Fruit Pancakes, Buckwheat, or Gingerbread Pancakes, this can be made up to two days in advance.

4 cups peeled and diced tart baking
  apples
Juice of ½ lemon
½ cup firmly packed light brown sugar
1 teaspoon ground cinnamon
⅛ teaspoon ground cloves
⅛ teaspoon grated nutmeg
1 teaspoon cornstarch
½ cup apple juice or water

1. Combine the apples, lemon juice, sugar, and cinnamon in a small, heavy saucepan. Place over medium heat, stir until the sugar is dissolved, and bring the mixture to a simmer. Simmer until the apples are crisp-tender, 5 to 7 minutes.

2. In a small bowl, combine the cornstarch and apple juice or water and stir until smooth. Stir in a few tablespoons of liquid from the pan, stirring until smooth, then stir this mixture back into the saucepan. Simmer the mixture until thickened, 3 or 4 minutes. Serve warm or chilled.

**Gingerbread Pancakes topped with
Apples in Brown Sugar Sauce.**

MORE PANCAKE TOPPINGS

Cinnamon Yogurt and Fruit Combine 1 cup plain nonfat yogurt with 2 tablespoons molasses, ½ teaspoon cinnamon, and ¼ teaspoon vanilla. Spread onto pancakes and top with sliced bananas, peaches, or berries.

Sweet Ricotta and Berries Combine 1 cup lowfat ricotta cheese with 2 tablespoons sugar, ½ teaspoon vanilla, ½ teaspoon grated lemon rind, and a pinch of salt. Spread onto pancakes and top with raspberries or sliced strawberries.

Honey Butter Combine ½ cup (1 stick) softened butter, ½ cup honey, and 1 teaspoon grated orange rind. Beat until fluffy, cover, and refrigerate until serving.

Maple Butter Combine ½ cup (1 stick) butter with ¾ cup maple syrup. Beat until fluffy. Cover and refrigerate until serving.

Orange Butter Combine ½ cup (1 stick) softened butter with 1 6-ounce can orange juice concentrate, thawed. Beat until fluffy, cover, and refrigerate until serving.

Flavored Maple Syrups Warm 1 cup maple syrup over low heat; remove from the heat and stir in any of the following: ¼ cup lightly toasted sliced almonds and ¼ teaspoon almond extract; grated rind of 1 orange; 1 teaspoon cinnamon and ¼ teaspoon vanilla extract.

Quick Fruit Syrups Combine 1 cup good-quality jam with ⅓ cup water and stir over low heat until is syrupy. Serve warm.

Warm Lemon Syrup Combine ½ cup sugar, 1 tablespoon cornstarch, 1½ cups hot water, and the juice and grated rind of a lemon in a small, heavy saucepan and bring to a simmer. Simmer until thick and syrupy, about 5 minutes, remove from the heat, and stir in ¼ cup (½ stick) butter and a pinch of nutmeg. Serve warm over pancakes with fruit.

A Fancy Dinner for Friends

FOR 8

Ԑຂ

I'm not much for too-fancy cooking at home; restaurant cooking is best left up to the restaurants. And even when I have a "fancy" dinner it's always more down-home than uptown. But that still doesn't mean I don't like to gussy things up once in a while. A nice meal of wonderful flavors, a good wine, good music, and some candles is something I started doing quite a few years ago when I lived in a tiny apartment on lower Fifth Avenue in Manhattan.

My traditional fancy springtime "bouquet" of tulips and artichokes in an old cut glass footed fruit bowl.

MENU

Wild Rice and Mushroom Soup

Cloverleaf Chive Rolls

...

Slow-Roasted Pork Tenderloin with New Potatoes and Onions

Scalloped Rhubarb

Steamed Asparagus with Lemon Butter

...

Salad of Spring Greens with Mustard-Shallot Vinaigrette

...

Caramel-Coconut Custards

Way back then, a few good friends (William Barnard, Fran Barnes, Tom Barnes, Irene Ladden, Dana Landry, Lindsay Miller, Ken Sansone, Linda Sunshine, and Janet Sutherland) and I decided to get together once a month for a "gourmet" dinner with a theme. Each month we would pair up and each duo would prepare a course, with the selection of the theme and the preparation of the main course being the host's responsibility. I was the host for that first springtime dinner. I don't even remember the theme, I'm sorry to say, but I do remember the decoration on my table, a bowl of tulips and artichokes. And "Tulips and Artichokes" became our name. Of course, as time went on, we all tried to outdo one another with themes such as "The Ides of March" and, of all things, "Blue." But we always ate well (well, almost always), and we always

had plenty of laughs and a great time.

Our group is scattered all over the country now, from Cambridge to Pasadena, but every spring, I still have a fancy dinner with a bouquet of tulips and artichokes, using some of our favorite recipes, to carry on the happy tradition of good food and good friends.

Getting Ready There's a lot going on here, so a little advance planning and good scheduling are key.

A day ahead, make the dessert and the soup, and marinate the pork (or make the pork completely in advance and reheat it before serving).

A few hours ahead, make the rolls (or make them well ahead of time and freeze them), then pare the asparagus and radishes and get the salad greens ready. Get the pork in the oven about an hour and a quarter before serving. Get the rhubarb ready and add it to the oven about 45 minutes before the roast will be done. Warm the soup and the rolls, cook the asparagus and radishes, and toss the salad just before serving.

Wild Rice and Mushroom Soup

ℰℯ

SERVES 8

This is easy to make as long as you have some well-seasoned chicken stock on hand (it's okay to use good-quality canned stock). The only thing that takes a bit of time is cooking the wild rice, but it needs little tending.

2 tablespoons butter
4 scallions, white and green parts, chopped
4 ounces morels, shiitake, or other "wild" mushrooms, thinly sliced
10 ounces button mushrooms, thinly sliced

¾ cup wild rice, rinsed well and drained
6 cups chicken stock
2 cups half-and-half
2 tablespoons dry sherry or Marsala
Salt and freshly ground black pepper
4 scallions, green part only, shredded

1. In a large, heavy saucepan or Dutch oven, melt the butter over medium heat. Add the scallions and mushrooms and sauté until golden brown, about 7 minutes. Add the wild rice and 2½ cups chicken stock to the pan, cover, and bring to a simmer. Reduce the heat to low and cook, barely simmering, until the stock is absorbed and the rice is tender, about 45 minutes.

2. Meanwhile, in another saucepan, bring the remaining stock to a simmer over medium-low heat. Gradually whisk in the half-and-half and continue to cook until the mixture thickens slightly, about 5 minutes.

3. Pour the liquid mixture into the pan with the rice mixture, stir well, and place over the heat. Stir in the sherry and bring the mixture just to simmering. Season to taste with salt and pepper and serve immediately, garnished with shredded scallions.

Cloverleaf Chive Rolls

ℰℯ

MAKES ABOUT 1½ DOZEN

Years ago, warm fluffy homemade yeast rolls made a regular appearance on everyone's Sunday dinner table. I don't bother with them very often, but they're worth a bit of extra effort every now and then.

1 cup milk
2 tablespoons butter
1 tablespoon sugar
¼ teaspoon salt
¼ cup sniped chives
1 envelope active dry yeast
2 tablespoons warm water
1 large egg, lightly beaten

A rich and aromatic Wild Rice and Mushroom Soup is garnished with shredded scallions.

2 ½ to 3 cups all-purpose flour
¼ cup (½ stick) butter, melted

1. In a small, heavy saucepan over medium heat, scald the milk. Remove the pan from the heat and stir in the 2 tablespoons butter, sugar, salt, and chives. Allow to cool to lukewarm.

2. In a large mixing bowl, stir the yeast and warm water together. Stir in the milk mixture, then stir in the egg. Stir in 1½ cups flour and mix well. Continue adding flour, ¼ cup at a time, until a soft, non sticky dough is formed. Add the chives and mix well.

3. Turn the dough out onto a floured surface and knead until the dough is satiny and elastic, about 5 minutes. Lightly oil the bowl, form the dough into a ball, and place it in the bowl. Cover the bowl with a damp towel and place in a warm, draft-free place until the dough is doubled in bulk, about 1 hour.

4. Have ready two lightly greased 12-cup muffin pans. Punch down the dough, turn it out onto the work surface, and knead for a minute or two. Pinch off small pieces of the dough and form them into small balls about ¾ inch in diameter. Place 3 balls in each muffin cup. Brush the dough with the melted butter, cover the pans with damp towels, and allow to double in bulk, about 45 minutes.

5. Preheat the oven to 425°F. Place the pans in the oven and bake until the rolls are golden brown, 12 to 15 minutes. *(The rolls can be made in advance, underbaked slightly, and frozen; reheat the thawed rolls for a few minutes on a baking sheet in a moderate oven.)* Serve the rolls hot with sweet butter.

The colorful main course—a wonderful sampler of favorite springtime flavors.

Slow-Roasted Pork Tenderloin with New Potatoes and Onions

SERVES 8

Don't get scared by the length of this recipe, it's really very simple. The end result, a succulent and well-seasoned roast, is worth it. If you'd like, the whole dish can be made a day in advance. Reheat in a slow oven and slice the meat just before serving.

Marinade

2 teaspoons salt

1½ teaspoons freshly ground black pepper

1½ teaspoons dried thyme

1½ teaspoons rubbed sage

3 bay leaves, crumbled

½ teaspoon ground allspice

Grated rind of 1 small orange

• • •

2 to 3 pork tenderloins, about 4 pounds total

4 large garlic cloves, thinly sliced

¼ cup olive oil

¼ cup dry white wine

12 medium new potatoes, peeled and halved

24 small white onions, peeled

1. In a small bowl, combine all the marinade ingredients and mix well.

2. Cut slits into the pork and push the garlic slices into the slits. Rub the marinade into the surface of the pork and wrap tightly with plastic wrap. Refrigerate for 4 hours or overnight.

3. Preheat the oven to 425°F.

4. Remove the meat from the refrigerator; wipe off the marinade and discard it. Pour the olive oil into a shallow roasting pan just large enough to hold it comfortably. Place the tenderloins in the pan and roll them to coat lightly with oil.

5. Place the pan in the oven and brown the meat lightly on both sides, about 5 minutes per side. Remove the pan from the oven and reduce the heat to 325°F. Pour the wine over the meat, cover the pan, return it to the oven for 30 minutes, and remove the pan from the oven again.

6. Meanwhile, place the potatoes and onions in a pan with salted water to cover over high heat and bring to a boil. Boil 5 minutes, then drain.

7. Arrange the hot potatoes and onions around the meat and continue roasting, uncovered, basting occasionally with the pan juices, until the meat reaches 160°F. on a meat thermometer, about 30 to 40 minutes.

8. Remove the meat from the oven and let rest 10 minutes before cutting into ¼-inch-thick slices. Arrange on a platter with the onions and potatoes and spoon the pan juices over all. Serve with Scalloped Rhubarb as a condiment.

Scalloped Rhubarb

ℨ

SERVES 8

Rhubarb is usually transformed into dessert, even though it's not a fruit at all. Here it appears as a condiment for roasted pork; try it with duck, turkey, or smoked ham, too.

> 4 cups diced rhubarb
> 1 medium red onion, coarsely chopped
> ¼ cup golden raisins
> ¼ cup orange juice
> 2 tablespoons fine dry bread crumbs
> 2 tablespoons sugar
> 2 tablespoons butter

1. Preheat the oven to 325°F. Lightly grease a shallow 1-quart baking dish. Arrange the rhubarb in an even layer in the pan, then scatter the onion and raisins over it. Drizzle the orange juice over all, sprinkle with the bread crumbs and sugar, and dot with butter.

2. Bake, basting occasionally with the pan juices, until the rhubarb is tender and the top is lightly browned, about 45 minutes. Serve hot.

Steamed Asparagus with Lemon Butter

ℨ

SERVES 8

> 1 pound thin asparagus, cut into 3-inch pieces
> 2 tablespoons butter
> Juice and grated rind of 1 lemon
> 1 tablespoon chopped chervil or parsley

Place the asparagus in a vegetable steamer over simmering water, cover, and steam about 5 minutes, or until crisp-tender and a vivid green. Drain the asparagus and rinse briefly to stop the cooking. Return them to the pan, add the butter, lemon juice and rind, and chervil. Toss well and serve.

SPRING GREENS

When spring greens are in, I let the market tell me what will go into my salad. Aside from a variety of early and tender young lettuces, here are a few I like to use, alone or in combination.

Arugula This is my favorite. I'm always quite content to sit down to a salad of arugula lightly dressed with a little oil and vinegar and nothing else. Arugula has small and narrow dark leaves and a pungent, peppery flavor. Remove the stems and wash the leaves well.

Dandelion Greens These bright green leaves with jagged edges are probably growing right out on the lawn. Choose small, tender leaves; the larger and older leaves can be bitter.

Mustard Greens Another narrow oval leaf with a pungent flavor. Small young mustard greens are good in salad, but larger, older leaves are better cooked (page 82).

Watercress Available in supermarkets year-round, this green with small roundish leaves has a sharp flavor; it's best mixed with more mildly flavored lettuces.

COLORED EGGS

Using colored eggs as part of Easter decorations and celebrations is an old tradition, but I like using them anytime during the spring. I always keep my eggs rather simple, dyeing them a single color and then combining only two or three kinds in baskets lined with straw, moss, or raffia.

Here's how to color eggs naturally, rather than using kits or food colorings. Use either raw eggs in their shells or emptied whole eggshells. (Prick holes at either end and blow the egg out into a bowl from one end.) The uncooked whole eggs need to be stored in the refrigerator, but the colored eggshells will keep indefinitely.

Baby Blue Place 4 eggs in a small, nonreactive saucepan. Add water to cover, 1 cup coarsely chopped red cabbage, and 1½ teaspoons white vinegar. Place over medium-high heat and bring to a boil. Reduce the heat to low and simmer 10 minutes. Remove the pan from the heat and allow to cool. If the color is not deep enough, refrigerate the eggs several hours or overnight. Remove the eggs from the pan, place them on absorbent paper to dry, and refrigerate.

Pink Follow the instructions above, but substitute the drained juice from a thawed 10-ounce package frozen raspberries (save the berries for another use) for the cabbage.

Yellow Follow the instructions above, but substitute 2 tablespoons ground turmeric for the cabbage.

Tortoiseshell This method can be used on colored or uncolored eggs. Peel the papery outer skins from yellow onions. For each egg, cover a 7-inch square of cheesecloth with a single, overlapping layer of onion skins, then place the egg in the center of the skins. Carefully pull up the corners of the cheesecloth, twist together to wrap the egg tightly, and tie with string. Place the wrapped eggs in a saucepan in a single layer and cover with cold water. Bring to a boil over medium-low heat and boil gently for 15 minutes. Remove the pan from the heat and allow the eggs to become just cool enough to handle. Unwrap the eggs and rub them lightly with vegetable oil. Allow to cool completely, then refrigerate.

Salad of Spring Greens with Mustard-Shallot Vinaigrette

U se a mixture of young greens torn into bite-size pieces: leaf lettuces (red or green), chicory, or Boston lettuce, and whatever greens are available at the market (see box, page 23), allowing a handful per person. Just before serving toss with the following dressing.

Mustard-Shallot Vinaigrette
½ cup extra-virgin olive oil
3 tablespoons red or white wine vinegar
1 tablespoon balsamic vinegar
3 shallots, finely chopped
2 teaspoons Dijon mustard
¼ teaspoon salt
¼ teaspoon white pepper

Shake all the ingredients together in a covered bottle or jar and let stand an hour before using. Shake again just before dressing the salad.

Caramel – Coconut Custards

MAKES 8

O ld-fashioned and "fancy," these individual custards look very pretty unmolded onto small plates and surrounded by their own caramel sauce. Garnish each serving with a nontoxic blossom or two, or a few red berries.

1 cup sugar
4 large egg yolks
2 large eggs
¼ teaspoon salt
Pinch of nutmeg
2 cups milk
1 cup (½ pint) heavy cream
1 teaspoon vanilla extract
⅓ cup shredded coconut

1. Place ½ cup sugar in the top of a double boiler over simmering water, and cook, stirring constantly, until lightly browned and caramelized, about 5 minutes. Spoon the caramelized sugar into 8 custard cups and quickly tilt and turn the cups so the caramel coats the bottoms. Set aside to allow the caramel to harden.

2. Preheat the oven to 300°F. In a mixing bowl (preferably one with a pouring spout), whisk together the remaining sugar, egg yolks, salt, and nutmeg until slightly thickened and lemon-colored. Combine the milk and cream in a heavy saucepan and scald over low heat. Very gradually whisk the milk into the egg mixture, blending well. Stir in the vanilla and the coconut.

3. Pour the custard mixture into the custard cups and arrange the cups in a shallow roasting pan. Pour hot water into the pan to come halfway up the sides of the custard cups. Bake until the custard is firm and just beginning to brown lightly at the edges, 40 to 45 minutes. Allow the custard to cool, then cover the cups with plastic wrap and chill thoroughly.

4. Just before serving, unmold each custard onto an individual dessert plate by placing the plate atop the cup and inverting quickly. Serve immediately.

Caramel–Coconut Custards are served decorated with delicate pansies.

Supper on the Lawn

FOR 6

୫୭

MENU

Mom's Salmon Cakes

Roasted Peppery New Potatoes

Creamed Peas
with Green Onions

Sautéed Cucumbers
with Dill and Chives

• • •

Orange Chiffon Cake

Stewed Rhubarb and
Strawberries with Ginger

Once the temperatures start nudging upwards and the first warm evening of the year arrives, I can't wait to have that first supper outdoors. This menu—a longtime favorite in my family—is what I always serve, and here's the story behind it.

When Mom was a young bride she invited my Aunt Minnie (Dad's sister) and Uncle Jerry over for supper one spring night. That morning, as Dad was leaving for the fields, Mom asked what he'd like for supper. "Salmon," he replied, and off he went. Salmon! Well, Mom now had a

There's no surer sign of spring than when the lilacs and dogwoods are in bloom.

problem. She had never fixed salmon before, and even if she knew how, where would she find it? Back in those days in rural Ohio there was hardly any place to buy fresh fish. But Mom used her head: A hasty consultation with her mother-in-law and a quick trip to the canned goods shelf at the grocer's in town proved helpful, and this is the menu Mom came up with, more or less. Supper was served outside under a big old weeping willow tree and now, half a century later, Mom's still making salmon cakes with creamed peas the same way.

Getting Ready The salmon cakes can be mixed and shaped early in the day and cooked just before serving. Or make them well in advance and freeze them; thaw them in the refrigerator, then reheat on a baking sheet in a moderate oven

The peas and the cucumbers are best if cooked just before serving, but they can be pared early in the day and refrigerated. The potatoes should be made just before serving; start them about an hour before.

The stewed rhubarb and strawberrries can be made a day or two in advance and stored in the refrigerator, or made well in advance and frozen; the cake can be made a day in advance if necessary, but no sooner.

What could be better on a warm spring evening than salmon cakes and creamed peas?

Mom's Salmon Cakes

ℰℬ

MAKES 12

Years ago in middle America, if you wanted fish for supper it came from a can. Mom still always uses canned salmon, but I've made these with fresh salmon, too. The flavor's a bit different, but either version is delicious.

    4 cups flaked cooked salmon (or two
        15½-ounce cans red salmon, skin and
        bones removed, with its liquid)
    1 cup fine cracker crumbs
    2 large eggs, lightly beaten
    ¼ cup finely chopped onion
    ¼ cup finely chopped celery
    ¼ teaspoon salt
    ⅛ teaspoon freshly ground black pepper
    Vegetable oil

1. In a mixing bowl, combine all the ingredients except the oil and mix well. Shape the mixture into twelve ½-inch thick patties. Place the patties on a plate or platter, cover with wax paper or plastic wrap, and refrigerate for 1 hour. *(The patties can be prepared early in the day.)*

2. In a large skillet over medium heat, heat a thin film of oil to sizzling. Cook as many patties as will fit comfortably in the pan until brown on each side, about 5 minutes per side. Remove from the pan and keep warm while cooking the remaining patties. Serve hot with creamed peas.

Roasted Peppery New Potatoes

ℰℬ

SERVES 6

I like potatoes just about any way at all, but these are especially good alongside a simple main course, needing no gravy or any other extras.

    2 tablespoons olive oil
    1 tablespooon butter, melted
    1 tablespoon cider vinegar
    2 shallots, chopped
    ½ teaspoon mild paprika
    ⅛ teaspoon finely ground black pepper
    Pinch of ground cumin
    Pinch of cayenne
    1½ pounds small red potatoes, peeled
        and cut into ½-inch slices

1. Preheat the oven to 400°F. Drizzle the olive oil, butter, and vinegar over the bottom of a small, shallow roasting pan. Sprinkle the remaining ingredients over the fats and lemon juice. Add the potatoes and toss to coat them with the fats and seasonings.

2. Place the pan in the oven and roast, tossing occasionally, until the potatoes are tender and very well browned, 30 to 40 minutes. Serve hot.

Creamed Peas with Green Onions

℅

SERVES 6

Creamed vegetables, once a staple of the American dinner table, seem to have fallen out of favor over the years. I still like certain vegetables creamed, now and then, and somehow, salmon cakes just have to be eaten with creamed peas. Here's a somewhat lighter version of the old-fashioned favorite.

1½ tablespoons butter
4 scallions, white and green parts, chopped
1½ tablespoons flour
1 cup lowfat milk
Salt and freshly ground black pepper
Pinch of nutmeg
3 cups shelled peas

1. Melt the butter in a medium, heavy saucepan over low heat. Add the scallions and sauté until softened, 3 to 4 minutes. Add the flour and stir until it's absorbed into the butter. Gradually stir in the milk and continue cooking, stirring constantly, until the sauce is thickened, 3 to 5 minutes. Season to taste with salt, pepper, and nutmeg.

2. While the sauce is cooking, place the peas in a vegetable steamer and steam over simmering water until crisp-tender and a vivid green (timing depends on the size and age of the peas but it should take only a few minutes). Stir the hot cooked peas into the sauce and serve.

Sautéed Cucumbers with Dill and Chives

℅

SERVES 6

Cucumber salads are a staple at my house, but every now and then I like to try something a little different. These sautéed cucumbers will be a nice surprise.

4 medium cucumbers, peeled
1½ tablespoons butter
2 tablespoons snipped chives
1 tablespoon chopped dill
Pinch of sugar
Salt and white pepper

1. Halve the cucumbers lengthwise and, using a small spoon, scoop out the seeds. Cut into ⅛-inch-thick slices. *(The cucumbers can be pared early in the day and refrigerated until cooking time.)*

2. Melt the butter in a nonstick skillet over medium-high heat. Add the cucumbers and sauté until they are crisp-tender, 3 to 5 minutes. Add the chives and dill, toss well, and season to taste with sugar, salt, and pepper. Serve warm.

SPRING CHORES

- Open all the windows and air out the house.
- Prune the trees and trim the hedges.
- Plan new plantings.
- Make the first trip to the nursery.
- Clean out the garden.
- Thatch and reseed the lawn.
- Prune the roses.
- Turn the mattresses.
- Check and repair fences, gates, and stone walls.
- Clean out the roof gutters.
- Wash the windows and put up the screens.
- Spring cleaning!

Orange Chiffon Cake

MAKES ONE 10-INCH
TUBE CAKE

Chiffon cakes were quite revolutionary when they came onto the scene in the 1940s, since they achieved their light but moist texture from using liquid shortening rather than solid. This version, with its delicate orange flavor, is the perfect foil for stewed rhubarb and berries—and it's simple to make.

2 cups all-purpose flour
1½ cups sugar
3 teaspoons baking powder
1 teaspoon salt
½ cup vegetable oil
5 large eggs, separated
¾ cup water
1 teaspoon vanilla extract
Grated rind of 1 medium orange
½ teaspoon cream of tartar

1. Preheat the oven to 325°F. Lightly grease a 10-inch tube pan, line the bottom with wax paper, and grease the wax paper.

2. In a large mixing bowl, sift together the flour, sugar, baking powder, and salt. Slowly beat in the oil, then beat in the egg yolks, water, vanilla, and orange rind.

3. In a separate, clean bowl, beat the egg whites until soft peaks begin to form. Add the cream of tartar and continue beating until stiff but not dry. Fold the egg whites into the flour mixture and transfer the batter to the prepared pan.

4. Bake the cake until the edges are lightly browned and a toothpick or cake tester inserted in the center comes out clean, 50 to 60 minutes. Cool the cake in the pan for 15 minutes, then remove it from the pan to a wire rack to cool completely. Dust lightly with confectioners' sugar before serving.

RUBY RHUBARB

Rhubarb (or pie plant, as it is also known) is easy to grow and is usually the first "fruit" of spring, even though it's not a fruit at all. There are generally two varieties available at the market, field rhubarb and hothouse (field rhubarb stalks have the deepest ruby color).

In late spring, we kids used to go out to the back of the garden where the rhubarb grew, next to a narrow bed of lilies of the valley, and we'd break off the brightest red stalks of rhubarb. Then we'd set ourselves down on the back steps with a salt shaker in one hand and a rhubarb stalk (but never the leaves or roots, which can be poisonous) in the other and munch away.

Nowadays I prefer rhubarb stewed or in pie (page 86) and I try to keep some on hand in the freezer. Fresh rhubarb is quickly perishable, so it should be used within two or three days of picking. To freeze rhubarb, simply cut the stalks into ½-inch slices, pack into freezer bags, and freeze up to 6 months; thaw in the refrigerator before using.

Stewed Rhubarb and Strawberries with Ginger

MAKES ABOUT 3 CUPS

Go ahead and double the recipe—leftovers are wonderful the next morning for breakfast with a toasted English muffin and a cup of hot tea.

7 cups trimmed, thickly sliced rhubarb
   (about 2½ pounds)
1 pint strawberries, hulled and halved
2 cups firmly packed light brown sugar
½ cup orange juice
1½ tablespoons finely chopped gingerroot

Place all the ingredients in a medium, heavy saucepan over medium heat. Bring to a boil, reduce the heat to low, and simmer until the rhubarb is tender, 20 to 25 minutes. Serve chilled. *(Can be made a day or two before serving and refrigerated, or made well in advance and frozen.)*

Stewed rhubarb and strawberries make a simple cake even more special.

Spring Fever Breakfast

FOR 4 TO 6

ℬ

MENU

Berries with Honey–Yogurt
Dressing

Country Ham–Stuffed Eggs

Smoked Salmon–Stuffed Eggs

Pepper Biscuits

Apple Corn Muffins

Blushing Grapefruit Juice

Hot Coffee

Back on the farm, the livestock were kept in the barn and stables all winter, but when it came time to be let out into the pastures again, they all just went crazy, making noise and jumping around, and, yes, almost dancing in the fresh air. (The lone exception was my horse, Maisie, who never got terribly excited or ever moved too fast for any reason at all.)

In springtime all creatures, man and beast alike, seem to go crazy, and I'm no exception. On a warm morning I'm ready to pack a late-morning breakfast to take outdoors to a won-derful spot. Here, breakfast is served by a brook, but any particularly springlike spot will do—next to a blossoming forsythia, on a hill with a view, or out on the lawn where daffodils are pushing their way up through the ground.

Getting Ready The night or day before, make the yogurt dressing, pare the berries, hard-boil the eggs, bake the muffins, and mix the juice. In the morning, make the biscuits, and while they're baking, stuff the eggs.

Pack the eggs in a shallow container on a bed of greens to prevent them from rolling over, and cover tightly with plastic wrap. Pack the berries and dressing in refrigerator jars or containers. Pack all this into a cooler along with a crock of sweet butter. The biscuits and muffins can be transported in a napkin-lined basket.

Berries with Honey–Yogurt Dressing

ℬ

SERVES 4

½ cup plain lowfat yogurt
2 tablespoons honey
½ teaspoon vanilla extract
¼ teaspoon salt
1 pint strawberries, hulled and halved
½ pint raspberries

In a small jar, combine the yogurt, honey, vanilla, and salt; stir to blend well. Cover and chill. In a separate jar or other covered containers, combine the berries and chill. Serve the berries with dressing drizzled over them.

On a warm spring morning, the bank of a free-flowing brook is the perfect setting for a picnic breakfast.

- Spring rains
- Rhubarb
- April Fool's Day
- Garage sales
- Spring breezes
- The blossoming of fruit trees
- Forsythia
- Newborn calves
- Planting the garden
- Tulips and daffodils
- Flying a kite
- Sitting outside at dusk
- Lilacs
- My birthday

Country Ham – Stuffed Eggs

MAKES 6 HALVES

3 hard-boiled eggs
⅓ cup finely chopped country ham
⅛ teaspoon dry mustard
2 tablespoons mayonnaise
Hot pepper sauce to taste
Paprika

1. Cut the eggs in half lengthwise and carefully scoop out the yolks into a mixing bowl. Add the remaining ingredients to the yolks and mash with a fork until the mixture is well blended.

2. Mound the yolk mixture into the whites and sprinkle the yolk mixture lightly with paprika. Place the eggs in a single layer in a shallow dish or storage container, cover, and refrigerate. When transporting the eggs for a picnic, keep them chilled in a cooler until serving.

Smoked Salmon–Stuffed Eggs Substitute finely chopped smoked salmon for the ham and omit the hot pepper sauce. Add 1 tablespoon snipped chives or chopped scallion and 1 teaspoon chopped dill. Omit the paprika and garnish with chives or sprigs of dill.

Pepper Biscuits

MAKES ABOUT 15 BISCUITS, DEPENDING ON THE SIZE OF THE CUTTER

2 cups all-purpose flour
1 tablespoon baking powder
½ teaspoon salt
½ teaspoon freshly ground black pepper
⅛ teaspoon cayenne pepper
¼ cup vegetable shortening
¾ cup milk
1 tablespoon chopped parsley

1. Preheat the oven to 425°F.

2. In a mixing bowl, sift together the flour, baking powder, salt, and peppers. Using a pastry blender or two knives, cut in the shortening. Add the milk and parsley and stir with a fork until the dry ingredients are just moistened and a sticky dough is formed.

3. On a well-floured work surface, pat out the dough to a thickness of ½ inch. Cut out the biscuits using a floured biscuit or cookie cutter. Place the biscuits on an ungreased baking sheet about 1 inch apart. Bake until golden brown, 12 to 15 minutes. Serve hot, or cool on a wire rack and serve at room temperature.

Apple Corn Muffins

MAKES 4 DOZEN MINIATURE MUFFINS

Southerners don't much like sweetened corn breads, but it's never bothered us Yankees. Apples, cinnamon, and honey give this version a nice mix of flavor and textures. This recipe really makes a considerably bigger batch than needed for this menu, but since these muffins freeze so well I always make the whole recipe to have plenty to stash away in the freezer.

    1 cup stone-ground yellow cornmeal
    ¾ cup all-purpose flour
    1½ teaspoons baking powder
    ½ teaspoon salt
    ½ teaspoon ground cinnamon
    ¾ cup milk
    ⅓ cup honey
    1 large egg, lightly beaten
    2 tablespoons butter, melted
    1 cup coarsely grated peeled and cored
        baking apples

1. Preheat the oven to 375°F. Lightly grease four twelve-cup miniature muffin pans.

2. In a mixing bowl, sift together the cornmeal, flour, baking powder, salt, and cinnamon. In a separate small bowl, stir together the milk, honey, egg, and butter. Pour the wet mixture over the dry ingredients and stir with a fork until the dry ingredients are just moistened. Add the apples and stir them in with a few strokes.

3. Spoon the batter into the prepared pan, filling each cup about two-thirds full, and bake until lighly browned and a toothpick or cake tester inserted into the center comes out clean, 15 to 20 minutes. Remove the muffins from the pan and serve hot, or cool on a wire rack. Serve with sweet butter.

Blushing Grapefruit Juice

6 TO 8 SERVINGS

Combine 1 quart grapefruit juice (pink or regular) with 2 cups cranberry juice cocktail. Serve over ice, garnished with sprigs of mint.

Light and elegant fare for breakfast after an early morning walk in the woods.

Weekend Lunch Under the Trees

FOR 4

MENU

Sardine and Sweet Onion
Sandwiches on Caraway Black
Bread with Grainy Mustard

Country Bacon and
Sliced Egg Sandwiches on
Farmhouse Potato Bread with
Leaf Lettuce and Mayonnaise

Cucumber and Radish Salad

Cherry Tomatoes

• • •

Butterscotch Brownies

Strawberries

Iced Tea

Come springtime, weekends around here start getting pretty busy. There's always some digging to be done in the garden, something that needs to be painted, and I've always got to make more than one trip to the nursery. There are usually house guests around, and I've always got an extra pair or two of gardening gloves ready (after all, there is no free lunch).

But that doesn't mean we can't stop long enough to have a nice lunch. Usually it's a pretty simple affair, sandwiches, salad, and fruit, and maybe a few cookies or brownies. When there's really no time, there are all kinds of good breads available at the bakery at the supermarket, but I like baking bread, so there's always a loaf or two in the freezer. The sandwiches are usually something easy to assemble and I always like to offer a little variety.

Getting Ready Breads, always at their best when they're freshly baked, can also be frozen without losing their fresh-baked flavor. Make them up to 2 months in advance, and when they are cool, wrap well and freeze them. Put the thawed bread in a moderate oven for a few minutes and it will be just as good as fresh-baked.

The brownies can be made a day in advance or well in advance and frozen. The hard-boiled eggs and the bacon for the sandwiches can also be cooked a day in advance; recrisp the bacon by arranging on a baking sheet and placing in a moderate oven for 5 minutes.

The salad can be made in the morning or just before serving; it takes only a few minutes. Wash the berries and tomatoes early in the day and store in the refrigerator. Slice the bread and assemble the sandwiches just before serving.

Caraway Black Bread

❧

MAKES 1 LARGE OVAL LOAF

Aside from sandwiches, I love thick slices of this bread spread with a little sweet butter as an accompaniment to hearty soups.

1 envelope active dry yeast
1 cup warm strong coffee
¼ cup dark molasses
¼ cup cider vinegar
¼ cup (½ stick) butter, softened
1 ounce (1 square) unsweetened chocolate, coarsely chopped
2½ cups rye flour
1¼ to 1½ cups all-purpose flour
1 tablespoon salt
2 tablespoons caraway seeds

1. In a large mixing bowl, stir the yeast and the coffee together until the yeast is dissolved.

2. In a small, heavy saucepan over medium-high heat, combine the molasses and vinegar and bring to a boil. Remove the pan from the heat, add the butter and chocolate, and stir until the butter and chocolate are melted and blended in. Allow the mixture to cool to room temperature.

3. Stir the saucepan mixture into the mixing bowl, then stir in the rye flour, 1¼ cups of the

Sandwiches, a pretty salad of crisp cucumbers and just-pulled radishes, and iced tea.

all-purpose flour, and the salt, forming a soft dough.

4. Transfer the dough to a well-floured work surface and knead the dough, adding more white flour as needed, until the dough is smooth and elastic. Form the dough into a ball.

5. Clean and dry the mixing bowl, and then oil it lightly. Return the dough to the bowl, cover with a clean cloth, and place in a warm, draft-free place until the dough doubles in bulk, about 2 hours.

6. Punch down the dough and knead it for a few minutes. Shape the dough into a long oval and place it in the center of a lightly greased baking sheet. Cover the loaf with the cloth and allow the loaf to double in bulk, about 1 hour.

7. Preheat the oven to 375° F. Bake the loaf until it is darkly browned and sounds hollow when tapped with a finger, about 45 minutes. Remove the loaf to a wire rack and cool.

Raisin Black Bread Add 1 cup dark or golden raisins to the dough at the end of step 2.

STACK 'EM UP — MORE QUICK SANDWICHES

• Meat loaf with thinly sliced onions and chili sauce on French bread or Pesto Potato Bread

• Roasted Peppers (page 53) with fresh mozzarella and a drizzle of olive oil on black bread

• Slivered prosciutto or country ham with sharp Cheddar, sweet onion, and honey mustard on a poppy seed hard roll

• Open-faced smoked salmon with cream cheese, thyme, and chives on black bread

• Liverwurst and and crisp bacon with chopped scallions and yellow mustard on potato bread

Farmhouse Potato Bread

❧

MAKES TWO 9 X 5 X 3-INCH LOAVES

While this country white bread doesn't really taste like potatoes at all, it's a great loaf for slicing for sandwiches and toast.

½ pound potatoes, peeled and quartered
1 package active dry yeast
2⅓ tablespoons (⅓ stick) butter, melted and cooled
2 teaspoons salt
1 tablespoon sugar
7 to 8½ cups all-purpose flour

1. Place the potatoes in a small saucepan, cover with water, and boil until tender, about 20 minutes. Drain the potatoes, reserving the cooking water, and mash them very well so they are smooth and lump-free. Allow the hot potato water to cool to warm (about 110°F.).

2. In a large mixing bowl, stir together 3 cups of the reserved potato water (add more warm water if necessary) and the yeast and let stand for about 2 minutes. Add the potatoes, butter, salt, and sugar, and blend well.

3. Add 7 cups of the flour, beating until well blended. Add a bit more flour if necessary to form a stiff but workable dough. Turn the dough out onto a floured work surface and knead for 2 minutes. Form the dough into a ball, cover loosely with a clean towel, and let stand for 10 minutes. Knead the dough until smooth and elastic, adding more flour if necessary to prevent the dough from being sticky.

4. Clean the dough bowl and oil it lightly. Form the dough into a ball, place it in the bowl, and cover the bowl with the towel. Place the bowl in a warm, draft-free place and allow the dough to rise until double in bulk, about 1 hour.

5. Punch down the dough and knead it for 2 minutes, then divide it in two. Form 2 loaves and place the loaves in 2 lightly greased 9 x 5 x 3-inch loaf pans. Cover the pans with the towel

MOM'S VEGETABLE GARDEN

During the the early spring, while Dad and his hands were out planting the fields, we four kids would help Mom with the enormous task of starting our half-acre vegetable garden. We'd dig up the earth by hand and begin the season's first planting with rows and rows of different kinds of seeds—onions, peas, lettuce, radishes, beans, corn, tomatoes, cabbage, carrots, potatoes, and pickles.

Once the first tender seedlings pushed their way up through the ground, we'd watch over them like mother hens, digging around them, mounding the earth, and hauling water to keep them nourished. The biggest job of all came when we'd hear on the weather report that a light frost was coming that night. We'd haul dozens and dozens of Mason jars way back to the garden and place a jar over each tiny seedling to protect it from the cold. When all danger of frost was gone, we'd have to haul the jars back into the house and get them all cleaned up again so they'd be ready in a few weeks for the produce from the garden.

In a month or so there'd be bushels and bushels of produce setting all over the kitchen floor to be put up—onions to dry, peas to shell, beans to snap, corn to be cut off the cob, tomatoes to stew, and on and on. By the end of the season, the cellar shelves were filled with hundreds and hundreds of jars and the big chest freezer was full. We'd eat everything up during the winter, and then, come spring, we'd start all over again.

and allow to rise until double again, just above the tops of the pans, about 45 minutes.

6. Preheat the oven to 350°F. Bake until the loaves are golden brown and sound hollow when tapped in the center with a finger, 40 to 45 minutes. Remove the loaves to wire racks to cool.

Pesto Potato Bread Substitute extra-virgin olive oil for the butter and add 3 tablespoons finely chopped basil and 3 finely chopped garlic cloves at the end of step 2.

There isn't an easier dessert to make—or a more popular one—than brownies.

Cucumber and Radish Salad

ॐ

SERVES 4 TO 6

I like the crunch of Kirby cukes, more usually used for making pickles, in this salad; ordinary cucumbers can be substituted, but the seeds should be scooped out first. This is a cinch to make as long as you remember to start it at least half an hour before serving to let the cucumbers drain.

    4 Kirby cucumbers, unpeeled and cut into
       ⅛-inch slices
    6 large red radishes, thinly sliced
    1 teaspoon kosher salt
    ⅓ cup mayonnaise
    2 tablespoons lowfat milk
    1½ teaspoons sugar
    1 small onion, coarsely chopped

1. Combine the cucumbers, radishes, and salt in a colander, toss well, and allow to drain for 30 minutes.

2. In a medium bowl, combine the mayonnaise, milk, and sugar and blend well. Add the cucumbers, radishes, and onion and toss well to coat the vegetables with the dressing. Refrigerate until serving.

Butterscotch Brownies

ॐ

MAKES 16 SQUARES

    ½ cup (1 stick) butter, melted
    ¾ cup firmly packed dark brown sugar
    1 large egg
    1½ teaspoons vanilla extract
    ½ cup all-purpose flour
    1 teaspoon baking powder
    ½ teaspoon salt
    ½ cup semisweet chocolate chips
    1 cup chopped pecans or walnuts

1. Preheat the oven to 350°F. Lightly grease an 8-inch square baking pan.

2. In a small, heavy saucepan, melt the butter over low heat. Remove the pan from the heat, stir in the sugar until dissolved, and allow the mixture to cool slightly. Stir in the egg and vanilla. In a small mixing bowl, sift together the flour, baking powder, and salt. Add the dry mixture to the wet mixture and stir until well blended. Stir in the chocolate chips and ½ cup of the walnuts.

3. Pour the batter evenly into the pan and sprinkle the remaining nuts over it. Bake until the top is golden brown and a cake tester inserted in the center comes out clean, 25 to 30 minutes. Remove the pan to a wire rack to cool, then cut into 2-inch squares.

MY UNPLANNED GARDEN

My garden is never perfectly planned the way the experts say it should be, and it never looks the same from year to year. For example, in the largest flower border there's an assortment of perennials, which tend to get moved around from time to time, along with a wide variety of colorful, long-lasting annuals. (I'm not a snob about annuals; their constant blooms please me, and they also cover up any "mistakes.") And I'm happy to let a few flowering weeds have their space, too. There's no theme or color scheme. As I add to the garden every year, I just go through the seed catalogs and make trip after trip to the nursery and wing it—whatever pleases me at the moment I spot it is what goes into the ground. I keep telling myself I should plan a little better next year so I don't have pink cleomes growing up right next to the same shade of bee balm, but . . .

I like most of the work to be in the garden itself, not in the planning. I still like to dig in the dirt, getting down on my hands and knees, just like I did as a kid. I'm not much of a hoe or spade gardener—I use my hands so I can feel the earth, its texture, moistness, and temperature.

And I'm one of those gardeners who always gets too enthusiastic. I overplant, even knowing that I'm doing it as I'm doing it. But it really doesn't matter. The garden always looks great to me, and I still get as excited as I always have, watching a rose bush burst into bloom, clipping a few zinnias for the kitchen table, snipping a handful of chives, or watching one of my tomatoes form, grow, and ripen on the vine.

Yellow coreopsis spills over a stone wall.

I like my flower beds to look a little wild.

Monarda (bee balm) keeps the bees happy.

An old rose blooms along the fencerow.

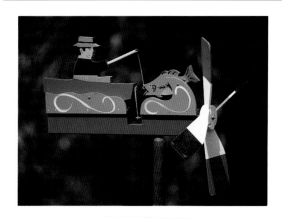

A Fisherman's Supper

FOR 6

ℰ

MENU

"Barbecued" Catfish

Hush Puppy Corn Sticks

Sugar Snap Pea Salad

Grilled Tomatoes with
Chopped Herbs

•••

Sour Cherry
Upside-Down Cake

Dad is the "old fisherman." All winter long, he putters about his boat, fixing and polishing, getting it ready for the next year. As soon as the first days of spring appear, the boat goes into the water for the season, and from that day on he can be found out on Lake Erie every morning by sunrise, catching walleyes, his favorite, and the justifiably famous Lake Erie perch. Then when he gets home he spends hours cleaning fish, a job he really enjoys. (Not me! I like "catching" my fish at the local fish market, already cleaned.)

This simple menu features farm-raised catfish, which are easy for us nonanglers to find in most grocery stores with a good fish department.

Getting Ready The dry rub mixture for the fish can be made anytime, as it can be stored indefinitely. Early in the day, bake the cake (the most time-consuming part is pitting the cherries; the cake itself is quick and easy). Anytime during the day, but at least an hour or two ahead, make the pea salad.

Since the corn sticks take very little preparation time, bake them just before serving, or no sooner than early in the day, if absolutely necessary. For the fish, step 2 needs to be done no later than an hour before cooking. Light the fire about an hour before you want to cook over it. The fish and tomatoes should be cooked just before serving.

Dad's never happier than when he's "pulling one in"(above). I'd rather cook it than catch it, and here's my idea of the perfect fish supper (opposite).

"Barbecued" Catfish

ℒ

SERVES 6

This isn't the usual "barbecue," but we always used to call anything cooked over an outdoor grill "barbecued." Here the fish is coated with a highly seasoned dry rub, quickly grilled, and then served with plenty of lemon wedges for squeezing. When grilling fish, I like using catfish, since the firm fillets hold up well on the grill. Any firm, thick, white fish fillet can be cooked this way, too.

Dry Rub

1 tablespoon celery seed
1 tablespoon dried thyme
1 tablespoon dried rubbed sage
1 tablespoon mild paprika
½ teaspoon cayenne pepper
½ teaspoon ground black pepper
½ teaspoon salt

...

¼ cup vegetable oil
1 large garlic clove, crushed
6 catfish fillets (2½ to 3 pounds)
3 lemons, cut into wedges
Flat-leaf parsley sprigs, for garnish

1. To make the dry rub, grind the celery seed in a spice grinder (or a coffee grinder wiped out

FISHING ON LAKE ERIE

Lake Erie has made a big comeback as one of the country's largest and most popular "fishing holes." Dad keeps his boat on Catawba Island, which is about halfway between the equally popular docking sites Sandusky and Port Clinton. The season for the best fishing on Lake Erie is a long one, from April into August. The most prevalent fish are walleyes, which, according to Dad, are swimming around just waiting for a hook to be plunged in the water so they can chase it and catch it. There are plenty of small-mouth bass and perch to be caught on Lake Erie, too.

A FEW GRILLING HINTS

• Before using the grill for the first time of the season, make sure the grill top itself is clean and, if it's a gas grill, all fittings are tight.

• Too much food has been ruined on grills because the heat source wasn't right. Before putting any food onto the fire, an even bed of coals should be covered in gray ash; this takes about 45 minutes from the time the fire is lit.

• Food to be grilled should be at room temperature to help even cooking.

• Use long-handled tools to prevent burns (the tools needed are a fork, turner, tongs that spring back on their own, and a basting brush) and use oven mitts.

• Always keep a spray bottle handy to spritz out flare-ups.

• Brushing the food to be cooked lightly with oil will help to prevent sticking.

well to remove any coffee particles). Add the remaining ingredients and grind together to blend well. Transfer the mixture to a small bowl or jar, cover tightly, and set aside. (*The dry rub can be made well in advance.*)

2. In a small bowl, combine the vegetable oil and garlic clove and let stand an hour or so. Coat the catfish fillets liberally with the dry rub, using your fingers to rub it well into the flesh. Wrap the fish in wax paper and refrigerate for an hour or so. Any leftover dry rub can be saved and stored for later use.

3. Prepare a charcoal or hardwood fire. When the coals are glowing and ash-covered, the fire is ready for cooking.

4. Brush the fillets lightly with the garlic oil and place them in a flat wire grilling basket. Grill the fish about 5 inches above the fire until it is opaque and will flake when pricked with a fork, about 5 minutes per side (the exact timing will depend on the heat of the fire and the thickness of the fillets). Serve immediately with the lemon wedges and sprigs of parsley.

Hush Puppy Corn Sticks

୨ଈ

MAKES 14

Hush puppies, those tasty nuggets of seasoned and fried cornmeal batter, are always great with fish. Here's an easier, just as tasty, but nonfried version.

1 cup stone-ground yellow cornmeal
1 cup all-purpose flour
1 tablespoon baking powder
1 teaspoon salt
½ teaspoon dried rubbed sage
3 tablespoons sugar
4 dashes hot pepper sauce
1 cup milk
1 large egg, lightly beaten
¼ cup vegetable shortening, melted and cooled
8 scallions, white and green parts, finely chopped

1. Preheat the oven to 425°F. Lightly grease 2 corn stick pans and preheat them in the oven.

2. In a mixing bowl, combine the cornmeal, flour, baking powder, salt, sage, and sugar and stir with a fork to blend well. Add the hot pepper sauce, milk, eggs, and shortening and stir until the dry ingredients are just moistened (do not overmix). Fold in the scallions.

3. Fill the pans with the batter until almost full. Bake until the edges are well browned and a toothpick or cake tester inserted in the center comes out clean, 15 to 20 minutes. Serve hot.

A late-spring bouquet of daisies and clover in an enameled metal bowl.

Sugar Snap Pea Salad

❧

SERVES 6

When sugar snaps are in season, I like having them often, hot or cold. The simple sweet-and-sour dressing for this salad is like that for a classic Midwestern bean salad.

Dressing
⅓ cup cider vinegar
⅓ cup vegetable oil
⅓ cup superfine sugar
1 teaspoon yellow mustard
½ teaspoon salt
½ teaspoon freshly ground black pepper
• • •
1½ pounds sugar snap peas
1 medium sweet onion, thinly sliced and
 separated into rings

1. In a small jar that has a cover, combine all the dressing ingredients. Cover the jar tightly and shake well. Refrigerate until needed.

2. Steam the sugar snap peas until crisp-tender, 4 to 5 minutes. Rinse with cold water and drain well. Transfer the warm peas to a bowl and add the dressing and onion. Toss well to coat the peas with the dressing, allow to cool, cover, and refrigerate for at least an hour before serving.

Grilled Tomatoes with Chopped Herbs

❧

This doesn't need a formal recipe. Simply cut firm, ripe tomatoes into ¼-inch thick slices, brush lightly with olive oil, and grill a minute or two on each side. Arrange the tomatoes on a serving platter and sprinkle liberally with whatever herbs are available and a generous grinding of black pepper.

An upside-down cherry cake, topped with whipped cream and toasted sliced almonds, is served on a Victorian cake plate.

Sour Cherry Upside-Down Cake

❧

MAKES ONE 9-INCH ROUND CAKE

Being a big cherry fan, I was happy to discover two old cherry trees on the edge of my property. Since I've now got plenty of cherries (as long as I get them before the birds do) and since I've always been a sucker for any kind of upside-down cake, this cake was inevitable.

3 tablespoons butter, melted
¼ teaspoon almond extract
½ cup sugar
½ teaspoon ground cinnamon
½ cup slivered almonds
1½ cups pitted sour cherries
• • •
¼ cup vegetable shortening
¾ cup sugar
1 large egg
1 teaspoon vanilla extract
1¼ cups all-purpose flour
¼ teaspoon salt
¾ teaspoon baking soda
½ cup buttermilk

1. Preheat the oven to 350°F.

2. Combine the butter and almond extract in a small measuring cup and pour the mixture into a 9-inch round cake pan. Tilt the pan to coat with the butter mixture. Sprinkle the sugar, cinnamon, and almonds over the butter mixture. Arrange the cherries in a single layer in the pan. Set aside.

3. In a mixing bowl, cream together the shortening and sugar, then beat in the egg and vanilla. In a separate bowl, combine the flour, salt, and baking soda. In thirds, beat this mixture into the wet mixture, alternating with the buttermilk.

4. Pour the batter evenly over the cherries. Bake until the top of the cake is golden brown and a cake tester inserted in the center comes out clean. Place the pan on a wire rack and cool 15 minutes, then invert the cake onto a serving plate. Serve warm or at room temperature.

Easy Saturday Night Dinner

FOR 6 TO 8

ℒ

MENU

Janet's Deviled Shrimp with Raw Vegetables and Toasts

• • •

Applejack Ham Steaks

Spiced Cantaloupe Pickle
(page 96)

Mom's Summer Chow Chow
(page 102)

Tomato and Herb Bread Pudding

Simple Pan-Fried Green and Yellow Summer Squash

Skillet Corn with Roasted Peppers

• • •

Plum Dumplings

Oil lamps and a few strings of quickly hung Christmas lights (opposite) transform the terrace into an enchanting dining spot.

In the summer, when we all let ourselves relax, without the constraints that cooler weather and being indoors seem to demand, everyone finds it less of a chore to entertain, and we want to enjoy the outdoors as much as possible. We've all got busy schedules on summer weekends, trying to take in all the pleasures (and chores) of the season. Dinner should be easy and not require a lot of time in the kitchen, and this menu was designed with that in mind.

Just about everyone has a favorite spot to eat outdoors — a deck, a porch, or even out on the lawn. Mine is the old-brick terrace at the back of the house, shaded by a towering black walnut tree and overlooking a flower border, the old oak tree down the hill, and the misty hills in the distance. On many a summer night after dinner on the terrace with friends, we can be found lingering: watching lightning bugs, listening to crickets and the owl who lives in the oak tree, and talking and laughing into the night.

GETTING READY FOR SUMMER

• Get back in shape to fit into that bathing suit!

• Get summer clothes out of storage and ready to wear.

• Make sure that the gear for summertime activities (fishing, softball, badminton, etc.) is in order.

• Get out the outdoor furniture — do any repainting or make any repairs necessary.

• Make a big batch of barbecue sauce.

• Plan a vacation!

• Pack the picnic basket with essentials (bottle opener, paper towels, matches, picnic blanket, trash bags, a sharp knife, a flashlight and batteries, plates, cups, and flatware).

Getting Ready Everything's worked out so only a few minutes' time in the kitchen is needed to get dinner on the table, and the earlier preparation is kept to a minimum. One note: During the summer all kinds of wonderful pickles and relishes are available at farm stands and farmers' markets, so you don't necessarily have to make your own. I usually have some of my own homemade pickles and relishes on hand in the cellar, and I've suggested two here that go particluarly well with the ham steaks. These can be made anytime in advance.

The pastry for the Plum Dumplings can be made well in advance and frozen or a day or two ahead and refrigerated. The dumplings should be baked no sooner than early on the day they will be served.

The ham needs to be assembled at least 4 hours before baking time; I usually do it the night before so it can marinate overnight. The bread pudding takes only a few minutes to assemble, but it can be assembled early in the day. Bake it along with the ham; put both into the oven no less than an hour before you want to serve.

The deviled shrimp takes only a few minutes, but it needs to be made a few hours ahead to allow the flavors to blend; it can be made up to a day in advance. Pare the accompanying vegetables early in the day, arrange on a platter, cover with plastic wrap, and refrigerate until needed.

Pare the squash and corn early in the day and store them in the refrigerator, wrapped well. Start cooking them simultaneously about 10 minutes before serving time.

Serve gin- or vodka-and-tonics as before-dinner drinks with the deviled shrimp, a fruity white jug wine on the rocks with dinner, and hot or iced coffee with dessert.

NEIGHBORS

Growing up on a farm outside a small town, my family and I knew everyone, everyone knew us, and everyone knew everyone else. We all knew each other's first names, knew families and their history, their joys and their sorrows, births and deaths. Neighbors gathered together for celebrations, and neighbors came together when someone had a problem and needed a hand.

Then I lived in New York City for twenty years, where people have good and true friends who may live fifty blocks away but may not even know the people who live in the apartment above them. It's not bad, it's just different.

When I moved out of the city, I didn't know what to expect. The world is a much busier place than it was when I left my hometown twenty-odd years ago and people don't seem to think of one another the way they once did. I

needn't have worried. On the day I moved in, Cathy, who lives down the hill, appeared at my front door with her little son Michael and a bottle of welcoming Champagne. And Vince, from across the road, dropped by to introduce himself and offer the use of his tools and gardening equipment "any time at all." Now we know one another a little better, and we do favors back and forth. Cathy came over a few weeks ago to ask my advice on the wreath she was making for her front door, and her husband, Ed, stopped by the other night with a magazine clipping about black walnuts that he thought I might find useful.

Robert Frost wrote that good fences make good neighbors. Well, there are no fences between us, but I do have good neighbors. It's nice to have neighbors again.

Deviled shrimp is served with toasts and sliced cucumbers in a big basket.

Janet's Deviled Shrimp

୨ଈ

MAKES ABOUT 2 CUPS

Here's a noncook recipe from my noncook friend, Janet Sutherland. (It's noncook if you use frozen cooked shrimp, thawed, which work just fine here.) Serve the spread with toasted thin slices of French or Italian bread (make your own toasts or buy them) and raw vegetables, such as cucumber slices, broccoli or cauliflower flowerets, or strips of bell pepper.

1 pound cooked shrimp
1 8-ounce package cream cheese, softened
½ cup mayonnaise
¼ cup chili sauce
2 tablespoons prepared horseradish
1 small onion, coarsely chopped
1 stalk celery, coarsely chopped
Juice of 1 lemon
1 tablespoon snipped chives
Hot pepper sauce

1. Combine all the ingredients except the chives and hot sauce in the bowl of a food processor fitted with the steel chopping blade. Pulse-process until the shrimp, celery, and onion are finely chopped and the mixture is well blended. Stir in the chives and plenty of hot sauce to taste.

2. Transfer the spread to a serving bowl or crock, cover with plastic wrap, and refrigerate 2 or 3 hours before serving. *(Can be made up to a day in advance.)* Garnish with chives or a sprig of parsley.

Hand method Chop the shrimp, celery, and onion very fine. Combine all the ingredients in a mixing bowl and beat with a wooden spoon until well blended.

Applejack Ham Steaks

ℒ

SERVES 6 TO 8

Nice and easy, and one of my favorite main dishes when I don't have a lot of time.

    1 cup apple juice
    ¼ cup applejack (additional apple juice
      can be substituted)

    1 tablespoon brown sugar
    1 teaspoon dry mustard
    4 ½-inch-thick ham steaks (about
      1 pound each)
    1 tablespoon grated gingerroot
    1 medium onion, thinly sliced

1. In a small bowl, stir together the apple juice, applejack, sugar, and mustard. Arrange the ham steaks in a single layer in a shallow, nonreactive baking dish. Scatter the ginger and onion over the steaks and pour the apple juice mixture over all. Cover the with foil or plastic wrap and refrigerate for 4 hours or overnight, turning once or twice.

2. Remove the baking dish from the refrigerator and bring to room temperature. Preheat the oven to 350° F.

3. Place the baking dish, uncovered, in the oven and bake, basting occasionally with the pan juices and turning once during baking, for 40 minutes, or until the steaks are glazed and browned. Serve warm.

Green and yellow squash surround Applejack Ham Steaks on an old Blue Willow platter.

Early tomatoes and herbs make this unusual bread pudding both beautiful and delicious.

Tomato and Herb Bread Pudding

ℬ

SERVES 6 TO 8

This recipe came about when I had the brainstorm that a summer pudding, which is merely layers of berries and bread and requires no cooking at all, might be made with tomatoes rather than berries. What could be more wonderful? The result was not wonderful and after two more tries, I gave up. The idea kept gnawing at me until I finally thought of changing the whole thing to a baked bread pudding. This time it was wonderful, and here it is.

3 cups chopped very ripe tomatoes
2 medium onions, coarsely chopped
¼ cup extra-virgin olive oil
1 tablespoon red wine vinegar
2 heaping tablespoons chopped oregano
   leaves *or* ¾ teaspoon dried oregano
1 tablespoon thyme leaves *or* ½ teaspoon dried thyme
2 tablespoons chopped basil (if fresh basil is unavailable, omit it rather than substituting dried)
½ teaspoon salt
½ teaspoon coarsely ground black pepper
¼ cup chopped black olives
8 to 10 slices firm, day-old white bread
1¼ cup lowfat milk
6 large eggs
1 medium tomato, sliced

1. In a mixing bowl, combine the chopped tomatoes, onions, olive oil, vinegar, herbs, salt, pepper, and olives and mix well.

2. Lightly oil a 9-inch round shallow baking dish or deep-dish pie pan. Line the bowl with bread, fitting the pieces neatly together so there are no gaps. Spoon a third of the tomato mixture over the bread, add another layer of bread, and repeat twice, finishing with a final layer of bread.

3. Combine the milk and eggs in a measuring cup, beat with a fork to blend well, and slowly pour the mixture over the bread, moistening all the bread. Allow to stand 20 minutes. (*The pudding can be assembled several hours in advance, covered with plastic wrap, and refrigerated.*)

4. Preheat the oven to 350°F. Arrange the tomato slices on top of the pudding. Place the bak-

ing dish in a larger shallow roasting pan and pour hot water into the roasting pan to come halfway up the side of the baking dish. Place in the oven and bake until the custard is set and the top of the pudding is nicely browned, about 40 minutes. Remove to a rack to cool and serve warm or at room temperature.

Simple Pan-Fried Green and Yellow Summer Squash

ℒ

SERVES 6 TO 8

The sprinkling of cheese adds a nice flavor accent without overpowering the squash.

2 tablespoons olive oil
1 small garlic clove, chopped
2 medium zucchini, diagonally cut into ⅛-inch-thick slices
2 medium yellow summer squash, diagonally cut into ⅛-inch-thick slices
1 tablespoon red wine vinegar
Salt and plenty of ground black pepper
2 tablespoons grated Pecorino Romano

In a large, heavy skillet, combine the olive oil, garlic, and squash and toss to combine. Place over medium-high heat and cook, tossing frequently, until the squash begins to brown but is still crisp-tender, 5 to 7 minutes. Stir in the vinegar. Season to taste with salt and pepper, transfer to a serving platter, and sprinkle the cheese over all. Serve immediately.

Skillet Corn with Roasted Peppers

ℒ

SERVES 6 TO 8

8 medium ears very fresh corn
1 tablespoon butter
1 roasted green bell pepper (see below), chopped
2 tablespoons milk
Salt and coarsely ground black pepper

THE BEST THINGS ABOUT SUMMER

- Being outdoors
- Roses
- Ice cream
- Vacations
- Swimming
- Casual get-togethers
- Sweet corn and tomatoes
- Picnics
- Combining (harvesting) wheat
- Lightning bugs
- Outdoor concerts and fireworks
- Frozen drinks
- Lemonade and iced tea with mint
- Watermelon
- Clambakes and barbecues
- Making hay
- Horseshoes and croquet on the lawn
- Flea markets
- Sunflowers

Scrape the corn kernels from the cobs, taking care to save all the milky liquid. Melt the butter in a skillet over medium-low heat. Add the corn and roasted pepper and sauté until the corn just begins to brown slightly, 3 to 5 minutes. Stir in the milk and cook 1 minute longer. Season to taste with salt and plenty of pepper, and serve.

Roasted Peppers

Preheat the broiler. Arrange the peppers in a large shallow baking dish in a single layer, skin side up. Place the dish about 4 inches under the broiler and cook the peppers until they are slightly charred, 5 to 7 minutes. Immediately remove the peppers to a plastic bag or small airtight container, close tightly, and allow them to cool. Remove the charred skins and cut up as needed. *(The peppers can be prepared up to two days in advance and stored in the refrigerator.)*

Chunks of juicy purple plums are wrapped in a free-form pecan crust.

Plum Dumplings

ℰ

MAKES 8

Pecan Pastry

1⅔ cups all-purpose flour
½ cup ground pecans (can be very
finely chopped by pulsing in a food
processor)
½ teaspoon salt
1 tablespoon sugar
⅓ cup (⅔ stick) butter, chilled
¼ teaspoon almond extract
4 to 6 tablespoons ice water

• • •

¼ cup sugar
1 teaspoon ground cinnamon
1 tablespoon flour
12 purple plums, quartered
4 tablespoons (½ stick) butter
Milk
Confectioners' sugar
1 cup sour cream

1. In a mixing bowl, sift together the flour, pecans, salt, and sugar, then cut in the butter until the mixture resembles coarse meal. Add the almond extract and 4 tablespoons water and work it into the flour mixture to form a stiff dough; add 1 or 2 tablespoons more water if necessary to hold the dough together. Form the dough into a ball, flatten slightly, and wrap in plastic wrap. Chill for 1 hour before using.

2. Preheat the oven to 425°F. Roll out the dough to a thickness of about ⅛ inch, and cut out 8 circles approximately 6 inches in diameter. Place the dough circles on a large baking sheet, letting the edges overlap slightly.

3. Combine the sugar, cinnamon, and flour in a small mixing bowl and mix well. Place 6 plum quarters in the center of each dough circle, sprinkle them with the sugar mixture, and dot with butter. Fold the edges of the dough over the plums, leaving a small opening in the center of each dumpling. Lightly brush the surface of the dough with milk.

4. Bake until the crust is golden brown, 20 to 25 minutes. Transfer the dumplings to a wire rack to cool, then dust them lightly with confectioners' sugar. Serve on individual plates with a dollop of sour cream on the side.

DOWN ON THE FARM

The Ohio farmland of my childhood (that's a "colorized" 1950s aerial view of our farm, above, and a snapshot of me and my horse, Maisie, above right) still holds magic for me. There you can find some of the most beautiful sights anywhere—rolling hills and lush flatlands—and there are a few sights that can bring on a chuckle or two, too.... There's no place like home.

Independence Day Ice Cream Social

FOR A CROWD

୨ଈ

MENU

Hot Fudge Sundaes

Butterscotch Sundaes

Strawberry Sundaes

Wet Walnut Sundaes

Strawberry Ice Cream
"Shortcake"

Spicy Oatmeal Cookie
Ice Cream Sandwiches

Frozen Fruit Pops

I scream, you scream, we all scream for ice cream." There's hardly anyone whose favorite dessert isn't ice cream in one form or another, especially in the summer.

Even with all the "gourmet" mass-produced ice creams available today, and even with all the varieties of frozen yogurt, nothing quite equals homemade ice cream, made with fresh cream and fruits. So a few times during the summer I splurge and make a few flavors of my own.

The Fourth of July is just about the best time there is to continue the old-time, all-American custom of the ice cream social. After a simple supper outdoors, I set up an ice cream "stand" on the terrace and let everyone dig in.

Getting Ready You probably won't make everything here for serving all at once, so first select your own menu. The hot fudge, butterscotch, and wet walnut sauces can be made well in advance and stored in the refrigerator. Homemade ice creams don't hold their freshly made flavor more than or week or two, so plan accordingly. Fresh fruit toppings are best made no more than a few hours before serving. The pound cake can be made a day in advance, or well in advance and frozen, tightly wrapped. Fruit pops can be made two weeks ahead.

At serving time, have all the "ingredients" ready for assembling all the ice cream concoctions. Make sure there are several ice cream scoops, a variety of ice cream dishes, and plenty of freshly whipped cream.

My own ice cream social (opposite), served on the back porch, is a scaled-down version of the ones held every summer at churches back home (above left).

Butterscotch, strawberry, and hot fudge sundaes in old drugstore sundae dishes.

Vanilla Ice Cream

୫ର

MAKES 2 QUARTS

I'm not one for gussied-up ice cream flavors— I like my ice cream pure and simple, with one predominant flavor rather than a conglomeration. So here's good old-fashioned vanilla, with a few fresh fruit and other variations.

    3 cups milk
    6 large egg yolks
    1½ cups sugar
    ¼ teaspoon salt
    3 cups (1½ pints) heavy cream
    4 teaspoons vanilla extract

1. In the top of a double boiler over simmering water, whisk together the milk and egg yolks. Gradually whisk in the sugar and then add the salt. Continue cooking until the mixture is thick enough to coat a spoon, 7 to 10 minutes. Remove from the heat and allow to cool.

2. Stir the cream and vanilla into the milk mixture, pour the mixture into an ice cream freezer, and freeze according to the manufacturer's directions.

Strawberry Ice Cream Reduce the vanilla to 1 teaspoon and add 2 cups coarsely chopped strawberries with their juice.

Black Raspberry Ice Cream Increase the sugar to 1¾ cups and reduce the vanilla to 1 teaspoon. Add 1 pint black raspberries, pureed and strained.

Blueberry Ice Cream Reduce the vanilla to 1 teaspoon. Simmer 1 pint blueberries with ½ cup sugar until the berries soften, about 7 to 10 minutes. Allow to cool, then add to the cream mixture.

Peach Ice Cream Reduce the vanilla to 1 teaspoon and add 2 cups coarsely chopped very ripe peaches and ¼ teaspoon each ground cinnamon and ground ginger.

Banana Ice Cream Reduce the vanilla to 1 teaspoon and add 3 very ripe mashed bananas mixed with 1 tablespoon lemon juice.

Cinnamon Ice Cream Reduce the vanilla to 3 teaspoons and add 1 tablespoon cinnamon.

Black Walnut Ice Cream Substitute 1 cup cooled strong coffee for 1 cup milk and stir in 1 cup lightly toasted chopped black walnuts.

Ice Cream Sundaes

Making a sundae is one of those "a little of this and a little of that" affairs and just about everyone knows how to assemble one, but just in case, here's how it goes.

1. Place 2 scoops of ice cream (using all one flavor is traditional, but go ahead and mix flavors if you want to) in a glass dish, preferably a tall, footed, old-fashioned sundae dish.

2. Spoon sauce (any kind and as much as you want) over the ice cream, then top with a big mound of whipped cream (for a professional soda fountain mountain of cream, pipe it on with a pastry tube fitted with a large star tip).

3. Add chopped toasted nuts if you'd like and top with either a fresh or maraschino cherry. Dig in.

SIMPLE FRUITY SUNDAE TOPPINGS

Strawberry Sauce Puree 1 pint strawberries with ⅓ cup sugar in a food processor or blender; add some sliced berries to the sauce if you'd like.

Raspberry Sauce Puree 1 pint raspberries and ¼ cup sugar together, then strain to remove the seeds.

Blueberry Sauce Simmer 1 pint blueberries and ½ cup sugar until the berries are softened, then cool; serve warm or chilled.

Sliced Bananas in Honey Add a splash of rum and a dash of cinnamon.

Hot Fudge Sauce

MAKES ABOUT 2 CUPS

For making everyone's favorite sundae.

2 ounces (2 squares) semisweet chocolate, coarsely chopped
¼ cup (½ stick) butter
3 tablespoons light corn syrup
⅔ cup sugar
¼ teaspoon salt
⅓ cup cold strong coffee
⅓ cup heavy cream
1 teaspoon vanilla extract

1. In the top of a double boiler over simmering water (or in a small, heavy saucepan over very low heat), combine the chocolate and butter. Stir until melted and blended.

2. Stir in the corn syrup, sugar, and salt, then the coffee and the heavy cream. Continue cooking, stirring constantly, until the sauce is thickened, 8 to 10 minutes. Remove from the heat and stir in the vanilla.

3. Allow the sauce to cool, transfer to a pint jar (or two half-pint jars), and cover with the lid(s). Store in the refrigerator.

4. To reheat the sauce, first allow the jar to come to room temperature. Place the jar in a small, heavy saucepan and add tepid water to the pan to come halfway up the outside of the jar. Place the pan over low heat and bring the water to a simmer. Continue heating, stirring the sauce occasionally, until the sauce is warmed, 5 to 10 minutes.

Variations Substitute any kind of whiskey for the coffee and add a pinch of grated nutmeg.

Add ½ cup chopped toasted walnuts or pecans.

Add 1 teaspoon peppermint extract when adding the vanilla, and stir in ½ cup coarsely chopped peppermint stick candy just before serving.

Stir in the grated rind of an orange and ½ teaspoon cinnamon.

THE CHURCH LADIES' CHICKEN SANDWICHES

Last summer, during a visit back home, some old friends and I went to an ice cream social at the Presbyterian Church in neighboring Plymouth. The menu hadn't changed much from the ones at the socials I remembered; along with the ice cream and its accompaniments, there were shredded chicken sandwiches, potato salad, and baked beans. I've never encountered shredded chicken sandwiches anywhere but back home, but I did manage to get hold of the recipe. Traditionally, the shredded chicken is spooned onto soft hamburger rolls, but I've made the sandwiches on toasted slices of Farmhouse Potato Bread (page 39), too. The recipe will make enough chicken for 4 to 6 sandwiches.

1 tablespoon butter
1 medium onion, finely chopped
1 stalk celery, including leaves, finely
    chopped
1 cup chicken stock
2 chicken breast halves
2 chicken thighs
1 tablespoon cornstarch
½ cup milk or cream

¼ cup very fine Ritz
    cracker crumbs
Salt and ground cayenne
    pepper to taste

1. Melt the butter in a medium, heavy saucepan over medium-low heat and add the onion, celery, and 1 tablespoon of the stock. Sauté the vegetables for 5 minutes, then add the chicken and the remaining stock. Bring to a boil, then reduce the heat. Cover the pan and simmer for 40 minutes, until the chicken is very tender.

2. Remove the pan from the heat and allow to cool slightly. Transfer the chicken to a work surface; remove the skin and pull the meat in shreds from the bones, discarding the skin and bones.

3. Return the meat to the pan and place the pan over medium heat. Bring the mixture to a simmer and reduce the heat to low. In a small bowl, stir the cornstarch and cream together. Stir this mixture into the pan and simmer 5 minutes.

4. Stir in the cracker crumbs and continue simmering, stirring and shredding the meat with a fork, until the mixture is thickened but still moist, about 10 minutes. Season with salt and pepper, then spoon onto warmed soft rolls.

Butterscotch Sauce

MAKES 2 CUPS

As a kid, I was always the oddball who liked butterscotch better than hot fudge, so I have to include this recipe for butterscotch sauce.

2 cups firmly packed dark brown sugar
½ cup light cream or half-and-half
¼ teaspoon salt
⅓ cup light corn syrup
⅓ cup (⅔ stick) butter
½ teaspoon vanilla extract

1. In a medium saucepan fitted with a candy thermometer, combine all the ingredients except the vanilla. Place over medium-high heat and bring to a boil, stirring constantly. Continue boiling until the mixture reaches 200°F. on the thermometer, 3 to 5 minutes. Remove the pan from the heat and stir in the vanilla.

2. Allow the sauce to cool, transfer to a pint jar or two half-pint jars, and cover with the lid(s). Store in the refrigerator.

3. To reheat the sauce, allow the jar to come to room temperature. Place the jar in a small, heavy saucepan and add tepid water to the pan to come halfway up the outside of the jar. Place the pan over low heat and bring the water to a simmer. Continue heating, stirring the sauce occasionally, until the sauce is warmed, 5 to 10 minutes.

Wet Walnuts

ℛ

MAKES 1½ CUPS

Here's the secret to making the gooeyest sundaes: Use the wet walnuts alone or with hot fudge.

- ½ cup firmly packed light brown sugar
- ½ cup granulated sugar
- 1 teaspoon ground cinnamon
- ¼ cup water
- ¼ cup white rum (see Note)
- ¾ cup coarsely chopped walnuts, lightly toasted
- ½ teaspoon vanilla extract

1. In a small saucepan, combine the sugars, cinnamon, water, and rum. Place over medium-high heat and bring the mixture to a boil, stirring occasionally. Continue boiling for 5 minutes, until the mixture is syrupy. Remove from the heat and stir in the walnuts and vanilla.

2. Allow the mixture to cool, then transfer to a pint jar. Store in the refrigerator.

Note: An additional ¼ cup water can be substituted for the rum.

"No-Nonsense" Pound Cake

ℛ

MAKES TWO 9 X 5 X 3-INCH
LOAVES

The traditional dish served at a Midwestern ice cream social is a "shortcake" made by topping a slice of pound cake with a big scoop of vanilla and fresh berries. It's even better if you toast the pound cake first.

This basic pound cake recipe can be varied in many ways, from adding a pinch or two of freshly grated nutmeg to the addition of currants, blueberries, or chocolate chips and chopped nuts.

- 2 cups (4 sticks) butter, at room temperature
- 2 cups sugar
- 10 large eggs
- 2 teaspoons vanilla extract
- 3 cups flour
- ½ teaspoon baking powder
- ½ teaspoon salt

1. Preheat the oven to 300°F. Grease two 9 x 5 x 3-inch loaf pans and dust them lightly with flour.

2. In the bowl of an electric mixer, cream the butter and sugar together until light and fluffy. One at a time beat in the eggs, then the vanilla.

3. In a separate bowl, sift together the flour, baking powder, and salt. A third at a time beat the dry mixture into the wet mixture, then continue beating at medium speed for 5 minutes. Divide the batter between the two pans.

Ice cream and strawberries in strawberry sauce top toasted pound cake for a Midwestern version of strawberry shortcake.

4. Bake for 1½ hours, or until the loaves are nicely browned and a toothpick or cake tester inserted in the center comes out clean. Transfer the pans to wire racks and cool 10 minutes, then remove the loaves from the pans, place them on the racks, and allow to cool completely. *(Pound cake freezes well for up to a month, tightly wrapped.)*

Spicy Oatmeal Cookie Ice Cream Sandwiches

☙

MAKES ABOUT 24 TO 36 COOKIES FOR
12 TO 18 SANDWICHES, DEPENDING ON
THE SIZE OF THE CUTTERS

The crunch and spicy flavor of these cookies make them go great with ice cream and they're perfect for making ice cream sandwiches. Most of the time I use pecans or English walnuts in the cookies, but when I make them in the fall I use some of my black walnuts. These make great sandwiches with fruit-flavored ice creams.

4 to 4 ¼ cups all-purpose flour
1 teaspoon salt
1 tablespoon baking soda
1 teaspoon ground ginger
1 teaspoon ground cinnamon
1¼ cups sugar
4 cups quick-cooking oats
1 cup molasses
1 cup vegetable shortening, melted and
    cooled

MORE ICE CREAM TOPPERS

• Toasted coconut
• A dusting of grated nutmeg and powdered instant coffee
• Coarsely chopped macadamia nuts
• Crumbled peanut butter or chocolate chip cookies, macaroons, or gingersnaps
• A tablespoon or two of liqueur

2 tablespoons hot water
2 large eggs, lightly beaten
1 cup finely chopped nuts
Sugar, for sprinkling

1. In a mixing bowl, sift together 4 cups flour, the salt, the baking soda, and the spices. Stir in the sugar, then the oats. In a separate bowl, beat together the molasses, shortening, and hot water, then beat in the eggs. Gradually add the dry ingredients to the wet mixture and knead to form a stiff dough, adding more flour a tablespoon at a time, if necessary. Add the nuts and mix well.

2. Preheat the oven to 375°F. Lightly grease 2 large baking sheets. On a lightly floured work surface, roll out the dough to a thickness of ¼ inch. Using a scalloped 3- to 4-inch cookie cutter, cut out the cookies and place them 2 inches apart on the baking sheets. Brush the surface of the cookies with cold water and sprinkle lightly with sugar.

3. Bake until the edges of the cookies are nicely browned, 8 to 10 minutes. Transfer the cookies to wire racks to cool, and store the cookies in tightly covered tins until using.

Ice Cream Sandwiches Cut shapes from 1-inch-thick slices of hard ice cream using the same cutter as used for the cookies. Assemble the sandwiches quickly, wrap in wax paper, and freeze.

All kids love ice cream sandwiches (left).

A root beer float (opposite) is no more than ice cream and root beer in a tall glass.

Frozen Fruit Pops

❧

MAKES 6 TO 8, DEPENDING
ON THE SIZE OF THE MOLDS

Fruit pops, the better-for-you alternative to gooey ice cream concoctions, are especially good heat and thirst quenchers on a hot day.

3½ cups fruit (sliced peaches, plums,
    bananas, or strawberries; whole
    raspberries; cubed cantaloupe
    or honeydew melon)
⅓ cup sugar
1 tablespoon lemon juice
½ cup water
Wooden pop sticks

1. In the bowl of a food processor fitted with the steel chopping blade, combine all the ingredients. Pulse-process to form a slightly lumpy puree.

2. Divide the mixture among ice-pop molds, filling them, and insert wooden sticks, if your ice-pop mold does not come with its own handles. Freeze according to mold directions.

THE GLORIOUS FOURTH

Hats off!
Along the street there comes
A blare of bugles, a ruffle of drums,
A flash of colors beneath the sky;
Hats off!
The flag is passing by.

Henry H. Bennett

America is a land of small towns and rural countrysides where people are still sentimental and patriotism still runs high. Here in Chatham, the Fourth of July is celebrated the way it's celebrated back in Willard, and just about everywhere else across the country. Somehow, the fact that, no matter where we are, we're all doing the same thing, makes it even better.

First thing in the morning, flags are raised to fly from porch posts and storefronts, car antennas and front yard poles (I even poke little flags into my window boxes), and then there's a big parade in town, with all the ingredients that make our hearts beat a little faster—bands playing marches by Sousa; antique fire engines proudly polished up to take their place alongside the new ones; Boy Scouts and Girl Scouts, horses and highlanders; Model T Fords and brand-new convertibles carrying local dignitaries; veterans and twirlers and floats; and even Betsy Ross and Uncle Sam.

The afternoons and early evenings are filled with get-togethers of families and friends, picnics and barbecues, and then the day ends with spectacular fireworks exploding against the stars to the excited shouts of the crowd.

Dinner for a Sweltering Evening

FOR 6

MENU

Frozen Pink Lemonade

Colby Cheese Crackers

• • •

Curried Carrot Soup

• • •

Jersey Shore Chef's Salad

• • •

Blackberry Summer Pudding
with Peaches and Cream

Last summer we had a heat wave, and I was having some friends over for dinner. It was so hot I didn't want to cook and for a moment I was tempted to order a pizza. Instead, I came up with this almost no-cook menu that starts with frozen drinks and continues with a cold soup and a cold salad as the main course.

I now have the perfect place to enjoy dinner on a hot night. When I moved into my house, out back there was a huge out-of-control border of forsythia winding around and in front of two rows of tall and ancient lilac bushes; up until only a few years ago, a chicken house stood there. Now some of the forsythia has been pulled out and the rest has been trimmed way back, and on the site of the old chicken house, sheltered un-

der the shade of the lilacs and an old oak tree, stands a screened-in gazebo, the perfect place to cool off with a cold drink and a cool dinner.

Getting Ready The idea here is for there to be almost no work, and certainly no heat in the kitchen before dinner. There's only a bit of actual indoor cooking to be done here, and that can be done well ahead of time. The crackers

can be baked in advance and stored in a tightly covered container. The soup can be made well in advance and frozen, or a day or two in advance and stored in the refrigerator. In any event, it doesn't take much work or time.

The berries for the summer pudding need to be cooked, and this should be done anytime on the day before the dinner; the pudding needs to

If this doesn't cool you off, nothing will.

be assembled the day before and refrigerated overnight.

The other bit of indoor cooking is steaming the zucchini, which can be done early in the day. Also early in the day, make the dressing/marinade, prepare the eggplant, marinate it with the zucchini, and marinate the swordfish. The swordfish and vegetables should be put onto the grill no more than an hour before serving, but if you'd prefer to have them cold they can be cooked anytime during the day.

An hour or so before serving time, prepare the greens, the other raw salad ingredients, the peaches. Whip the cream just before serving.

The frozen lemonade should be whirred up in the blender immediately before serving, but this is no work at all.

With the cold soup and cool and warm main-course salad, I like to serve icy lager beer, and on a hot night, iced coffee with dessert.

Frozen Pink Lemonade

MAKES 6 DRINKS

I like to make my own lemonade most of the time, since it's so easy. But there are times, and a blistering day is one of them, when I'm much happier reaching into the freezer for one of those little cans. In any case, the frozen concentrate fits the bill for making frozen drinks.

Fill the container of a blender to about ⅔ full with small ice cubes. Add a 6-ounce can of frozen pink lemonade concentrate and a canful of white rum or tequila and blend away. Pour into slender wine glasses and garnish with a twist of lemon or lime.

Colby Cheese Crackers

MAKES ABOUT 4 DOZEN

Ohio Colby cheese could always be found in our icebox when I was growing up and I'm still partial to its mellow Cheddar-like flavor. These slightly spicy crackers make a nice partner for icy-cold drinks. I usually make a double or triple batch to keep some on hand in the freezer.

1½ cups (about 6 ounces) grated
    Colby cheese
½ cup (1 stick) butter, softened
¾ cup all-purpose flour
¼ cup stone-ground yellow cornmeal
¼ teaspoon dry mustard
¼ teaspoon freshly ground black pepper
1 to 2 tablespooons milk
1 tablespoon snipped chives

1. In a mixing bowl, beat the cheese and butter together until well blended. In a separate bowl, sift together the flour, cornmeal, mustard, and pepper. Gradually beat the flour mixture into the cheese mixture until well blended. Beat in just enough milk to form a soft dough. Add the chives and blend well.

2. Turn the dough out onto a lightly floured surface and shape it into a cylinder about 1 inch in diameter, then flatten the cylinder slightly. Wrap the dough in plastic wrap and refrigerate until firm, 3 to 4 hours. *(The dough can be made up to two days in advance, or it can be wrapped well and frozen for up to two months; thaw in the refrigerator before proceeding.)*

3. Preheat the oven to 400°F. Cut the dough cylinder into ⅛-inch-thick slices. Place the slices on an ungreased baking sheet about 1 inch apart and prick the slices with a fork. Bake until the edges of the crackers are lightly browned, 12 to 15 minutes.

4. Transfer the crackers to wire racks to cool, then store in tightly covered containers up to two weeks. (In humid weather, the crackers may need to be recrisped; arrange in a single layer on a baking sheet and place in a 250°F. oven for 2 or 3 minutes.)

COOLING OFF ON A SUMMER NIGHT

Back in the days before everything was air-conditioned, the best way to cool off after a hot day spent out in the fields was to go for a ride in the car after sunset with all the windows open. We'd always take the back roads so Dad could keep up-to-date by seeing what the other farmers in our area were doing. The "surprise" destination for a good many of our evening rides turned out to be the tiny town of Siam, where an old farm couple sold their own homemade ice cream at a little roadside stand. My very favorite flavor was black raspberry, made only during raspberry season. My other favorites were black walnut and a marbly butterscotch.

None of the fancy and pricey gourmet ice creams around can even come close to that ice cream made with fresh cream and just-picked fruits, and somehow, even air-conditioning never seems to cool me off as well as a breezy nighttime ride in the country.

Curried Carrot Soup

SERVES 6 TO 8

Just a hint of curry tempers the natural sweetness of the carrots in this refreshing cool soup.

2 tablespoons butter
1 medium onion, coarsely chopped
1 stalk celery with leaves, coarsely chopped
1 large garlic clove, chopped
1½ pounds carrots, peeled and sliced
2 medium potatoes, peeled and quartered
4 cups well-seasoned chicken stock
½ teaspoon salt
1 teaspoon good-quality curry powder
1½ cups lowfat yogurt
Pinch of cayenne pepper
Snipped chives, for garnish

1. Melt the butter in a Dutch oven or large, heavy saucepan over medium heat. Add the onion, celery, and garlic and sauté until the onion is golden, 5 to 7 minutes.

2. Add the carrots, potatoes, stock, and salt to the pan, raise the heat to medium-high, and bring the mixture to a boil. Reduce the heat, cover the pan, and simmer until the carrots are very tender, about 30 minutes. Remove the pan from the heat, stir in the curry powder, and allow the mixture to cool slightly.

3. In a blender or in the bowl of a food processor fitted with the steel chopping blade, blend or process the mixture to a lumpy puree. Transfer the soup to a large bowl, then stir in 1 cup yogurt and season to taste with salt and cayenne. Cool, cover, and chill until serving. *(Can be made up to two days in advance or can be made well in advance and frozen.)*

4. Serve the soup in shallow bowls and garnish each serving with an additional dollop of yogurt and a sprinkling of snipped chives.

Warm grilled swordfish and vegetables top a cool bed of crisp greens.

Jersey Shore Chef's Salad

❧

SERVES 6

Marinade/Dressing

⅔ cup olive oil

Juice of 1 orange

3 tablespoons red wine vinegar

2 tablespoons soy sauce

1 bunch scallions, white and green parts, finely chopped

2 large garlic cloves, finely chopped

•••

1 medium eggplant

Salt

3 medium zucchini

3 1-inch-thick swordfish steaks (about 2¼ pounds)

4 cups leaf lettuce in bite-size pieces

1 bunch arugula

1 small red onion, sliced and separated into rings

½ cup pitted black olives

2 oranges, sectioned

1 large or 2 medium ripe tomatoes, cut into wedges

1. In a jar with a lid, combine the marinade/dressing ingredients. Cover, shake well, and refrigerate. *(Can be made a day in advance.)*

2. Peel the eggplant and cut it into 1-inch cubes. Sprinkle the eggplant lightly with salt, place in a colander, and set over a bowl for 30 minutes to drain.

3. Cut the zucchini into 1-inch thick slices. Place in a steamer basket over boiling water and steam 5 minutes. Cool.

4. Combine the eggplant and zucchini in a bowl and pour ⅔ of the dressing over the vegetables. Toss to coat the vegetables with the dressing. Cut the swordfish steaks into 1-inch cubes and combine in a bowl with the remaining dressing. Refrigerate both mixtures at least 1 hour. *(Can be prepared up to 6 hours before cooking)*.

5. Prepare a charcoal fire. The fire is ready when all flames have died down and the coals are glowing and just covered with gray ash.

6. On 6 to 8 skewers, alternately skewer the swordfish, eggplant, and zucchini. Reserve the two bowls of marinade.

7. Place the skewers on the grill about 2 inches above the coals and cook until well browned, 3 to 4 minutes per side. Brush occasionally with any remaining marinade from the swordfish. Remove the skewers from the grill and reserve.

8. Arrange the lettuce and arugula on a large serving platter or large shallow bowl. Scatter the onion rings, olives, orange slices, and tomatoes over the greens, then pour the reserved marinade from the vegetables over all. Arrange the skewered fish and vegetables on the salad and serve.

Blackberry Summer Pudding with Peaches and Cream

ॐ

SERVES 6 TO 8

The beautiful colors and intensely fruity flavors in this dessert really lift the spirits on a hot summer night. The added bonus for the cook is that it requires only about 10 minutes of actual cooking. If you can't get blackberries, don't just skip this one—red or black raspberries are more than adequate substitutes.

3 cups (1½ pints) blackberries
1¼ cups sugar
½ cup apple juice
1 loaf firm, dense sliced white bread, crusts removed
2 cups sliced peaches tossed with 2 teaspoons lemon juice
½ pint heavy cream, whipped
2 peaches, peeled and sliced

1. In a heavy saucepan, combine the berries (reserve a few for use as a garnish), sugar, and apple juice. Bring to a simmer and cook over low heat, stirring occasionally, until the sugar is dissolved and the liquid bcomes syrupy, about 10 minutes. Remove from the heat and allow to cool.

2. Lightly oil a round, deep bowl (about 2 quarts). Line the bowl with bread, fitting the pieces neatly together so there are no gaps. Spoon half the berries over the bread. Add another layer of bread, then spoon the remaining berries over it. Top with a final layer of bread.

3. Cover the top layer of bread with a plate that's slightly smaller than the bowl and weight down the plate (a few canned goods work well). Refrigerate for 8 hours or overnight.

4. Just before serving, invert the pudding onto a serving plate that has a lip to catch any juices. Surround the pudding with the sliced peaches and the reserved berries and top it with a big dab of whipped cream. Cut the pudding into thin wedges to serve.

After dark, a cool dessert is served on an old glass cakestand in the glow of gas lanterns.

A Blue Ribbon Picnic

FOR 8

❧

MENU

Ohio Pan-Fried Chicken

Mashed Potato Salad

Dilly Bean Salad

Cabbage and Zucchini Slaw

Sliced Jersey Tomatoes with
Sweet Mustard Dressing

Corn Relish Muffins

• • •

Nectarine Cake

Iced Herbal Tea with Lemon

**An old apple orchard was the perfect
place for a late-afternoon picnic.**

A simple bouquet arranged in an unbreakable pitcher is easy to transport.

During the course of the summer, there are plenty of excuses for packing a lunch or supper, from a concert in the park to the annual town picnic or from a local Little League game or canoe race to the county or state fair. Here's a menu that uses some of the best of summer produce in dishes that require little fuss to make and can travel easily.

Getting Ready It's much nicer to use real plates, glasses, and utensils (for your guests and for the environment) rather than plastic and paper. I use inexpensive, sturdy glasses and heavy earthenware dishes, nothing fancy or expensive. Wrap any breakables in the tablecloth and napkins and pack them snugly into the picnic basket to help avoid breakage.

The potato salad, bean salad, slaw, and dressing for the tomatoes can be made a day in advance. Pack them in jars or containers that are easy to transport in a cooler; if the containers are glass, wrap napkins or towels around them to avoid breakage. The cake, too, can be made a day in advance. Transport it in the pan, covered tightly with plastic wrap.

The chicken can be made a day in advance if need be, but it's best if made no sooner than early on the day it's to be served. Pack it in a towel- or napkin-lined basket, cover, and transport in the cooler.

The muffins should be made no sooner than early in the day, but they can be made pretty quickly. Pack them in a napkin-lined basket, then wrap tightly with foil to keep them fresh.

I carry tea in a large jar with a carrying handle and pack ice separately in the cooler, but the tea can also be carried in an insulated jug.

Ohio Pan-Fried Chicken

⌘

MAKES 16 PIECES

This way of fixing fried chicken—browning it first in a skillet, then finishing the cooking in the oven—comes from Holmes County, Ohio, the largest Amish community in the country. The chicken comes out moist and tender inside and crispy but light on the outside. Delicious.

2 large eggs, lightly beaten
1¼ cups buttermilk
3 garlic cloves, finely chopped
½ cup stone-ground yellow cornmeal
½ cup all-purpose flour
1 teaspoon salt
1 teaspoon freshly ground black pepper
1 teaspoon paprika
2 frying chickens (about 3 pounds each),
  cut into eighths
Vegetable shortening, for frying

1. In a large shallow dish, combine the eggs, buttermilk, and garlic. Cover tightly and refrigerate 3 hours or overnight.

2. In a shallow bowl, combine the cornmeal, flour, salt, pepper, and paprika and blend well. Reserve. A piece at a time, dip the chicken in the buttermilk mixture, then roll in the cornmeal mixture to coat well on all sides. Cover with wax paper and refrigerate for 1 hour.

3. In a large, heavy skillet over medium heat, melt enough shortening to reach a depth of ⅛ inch. A few pieces at a time, sauté the chicken until lightly browned on all sides.

4. Preheat the oven to 350°F. Arrange the chicken pieces in a single layer, skin side up, on a baking sheet. Bake until the chicken is well browned and the juices run clear when pricked with a fork, 30 to 40 minutes. Allow the chicken to cool completely before refrigerating it so the outside remains crisp. Serve at room temperature.

Fried chicken, sliced tomatoes, and a potluck assortment of favorite summertime salads.

Mashed Potato Salad

&

SERVES 8

Anybody who knows me at all knows I'm a potato salad nut; during the summer, hardly a weekend goes by without it showing up on the table in one form or another. Mashed potato salad is a classic Midwestern variation and an old favorite of mine, and it's also one of the easiest things in the world to make. (And it's a lifesaver on those occasions when I'm boiling potatoes for salad and get distracted with some other chore, and—oops, the potatoes are too overcooked to be sliced!)

⅔ cup mayonnaise
2 tablespoons olive oil
2 tablespoons cider or wine vinegar
1 teaspoon dry mustard
3 tablespoons chopped parsley
½ teaspoon salt
½ teaspoon coarsely ground black pepper
3 pounds potatoes, peeled, boiled, and
    mashed by hand (leave a few lumps)
½ cup chopped red and/or green bell
    pepper
¾ cup diced celery
4 scallions, white and green parts,
    chopped
2 hard-boiled eggs, coarsely chopped

In a large bowl, combine the mayonnaise, olive oil, vinegar, mustard, parsley, salt, and pepper and stir to blend. Add the remaining ingredients and mix well. Refrigerate until serving.

Dilly Bean Salad

&

SERVES 6 TO 8

Try using a combination of green and wax beans; or add a handful of kidney beans, too.

¼ cup olive oil
2 tablespoons red or white wine vinegar
Juice of ½ lemon
2 teaspoons chopped dill
1 garlic clove, finely chopped
¼ teaspoon salt
¼ teaspoon freshly ground black
    pepper
1 tablespoon sugar
1½ pounds thin green beans, trimmed
1 small red onion, coarsely chopped

1. In a jar with a lid, combine the olive oil, vinegar, lemon juice, dill, garlic, salt, pepper, and sugar. Cover the jar tightly and shake well.

2. Bring a large pot of salted water to a rolling boil and add the beans. Cook the beans until they just begin to get tender, about 7 minutes. Drain, rinse with cold water, and drain again.

3. Combine the dressing, beans, and onion in a bowl and toss to coat the vegetables well. Allow the beans to cool, then refrigerate for 2 or 3 hours before serving.

Cabbage and Zucchini Slaw

&

SERVES 6 TO 8

Here's one more way to use up some of that zucchini that, come August, seems to be in endless supply from the garden.

Dressing
¼ cup mayonnaise
¼ cup olive oil
¼ cup cider vinegar
1 teaspoon dry mustard
¼ cup chopped parsley
½ teaspoon celery seed
1 teaspoon sugar
¼ teaspoon salt
⅛ teaspoon ground black pepper

•••

4 cups coarsely shredded red and/or
    green cabbage
2 cups julienned zucchini

Combine the dressing ingredients in a small jar, cover tightly, and shake well. Combine the cabbage and zucchini in a large bowl. Add the dressing, toss well, and refrigerate for at least 3 or 4 hours before serving.

Muffins travel easily and look great wrapped up in a colorful bandana.

Sweet Mustard Dressing

ℐℛ

MAKES 1 CUP

Drizzle just a little bit of this dressing over thickly sliced ripe tomatoes.

½ cup olive oil
¼ cup white wine vinegar
2 tablespoons prepared grainy mustard
2 tablespoons honey
¼ teaspoon salt
1 tablespoon grated onion

Combine all the ingredients in a jar, cover tightly, and shake well. Refrigerate overnight. Shake again before using.

Corn Relish Muffins

ℐℛ

MAKES 1 DOZEN

These aren't true "corn muffins," since they have only a bit of cornmeal in the batter, but they do have kernels of corn, along with bits of pepper and onion. The relish is easy to make, but you can also use a good store-bought kind.

1½ cups all-purpose flour
½ cup stone-ground yellow cornmeal
1 tablespoon baking powder
1 teaspoon salt
¼ teaspoon freshly ground black
    pepper
2 tablespoons sugar
2 large eggs, lightly beaten
1 cup milk
½ cup (1 stick) butter, melted
½ cup well-drained Freezer Corn Relish
    (page 96)

1. Preheat the oven to 400°F. Lightly grease a 12-cup muffin pan.

2. In a mixing bowl, sift together the flour, cornmeal, baking powder, salt, pepper, and sugar. In a separate bowl, combine the eggs, milk, and butter. Pour the wet mixture over the dry ingredients and stir with a fork until the dry ingredients are just moistened. Stir in the relish.

3. Spoon the batter into the prepared muffin pan, filling each cup about ⅔ full. Bake until the muffins are golden brown and a toothpick or cake tester inserted in a muffin comes out clean, about 20 minutes. Serve hot or at room temperature.

The nectarine cake's cinnamony glaze glistens in the late afternoon sunlight.

Nectarine Cake

MAKES ONE 10-INCH ROUND CAKE

1¼ cups all-purpose flour
½ cup plus 2 tablespoons sugar
1¼ teaspoons baking powder
½ teaspoon salt
¼ cup (½ stick) butter
1 large egg
½ cup milk
1 teaspoon vanilla extract
4 nectarines, peeled and sliced into eighths
1 tablespoon brown sugar
½ teaspoon ground cinnamon
½ teaspoon ground ginger

Topping

1 nectarine, peeled and chopped
½ cup sugar
¼ teaspoon almond extract

1. Preheat the oven to 350°F. Lightly grease an ovenproof glass or ceramic 10-inch round cake pan or pie pan.

2. In a mixing bowl, combine the flour, ½ cup sugar, baking powder, and salt, then cut in the butter with a pastry blender or two knives. In a separate bowl, beat together the egg, milk, and vanilla, then stir the wet mixture into the dry mixture, blending until the dry ingredients are just moistened.

3. Pour the batter into the prepared pan and arrange the nectarine slices in a circular pattern on the batter. In a small bowl, combine the remaining 2 tablespoons sugar, the brown sugar, and the spices, then sprinkle this mixture over the fruit.

4. Bake until the cake is lightly browned and a toothpick or cake tester inserted in the center comes out clean, 30 to 35 minutes. Transfer the pan to a wire rack and allow to cool before adding the topping.

5. To make the topping, combine the chopped nectarine and sugar in a small, heavy saucepan over medium heat. Cook, stirring constantly, until the sugar is dissolved and the mixture is syrupy, about 7 minutes. Remove from the heat and stir in the almond extract. Spoon the topping over the cake and allow it to cool before serving.

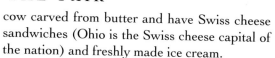

A TRIP TO THE FAIR

Just about every county and state has a fair to show off the best they have to offer. I've been going to the Ohio State Fair (the largest fair in the world) since before I could walk. Every year, on the fair's opening day, as soon as the cows were milked at dawn, Mom and Dad would pack us all into the car and off to Columbus we'd go. The day was packed with the judging of produce and cannned goods and baked goods and of 4H-ers showing their cattle, pigs, sheep, and horses. And of course, Dad always had to carefully inspect the displays of all the latest farming equipment, which bored us kids to death.

At noon we'd stop to wolf down the picnic lunch Mom had packed, but to us kids, the highlight of the day was a suppertime visit to the Dairy Association Building to see the life-size cow carved from butter and have Swiss cheese sandwiches (Ohio is the Swiss cheese capital of the nation) and freshly made ice cream.

Last summer I made my first visit to the fair in almost twenty years. Well, the fair's a lot slicker now (even the all-state youth band wore hats bearing the name of a pizza company!), but even modern-day commercialism can't change certain things. We saw the same rich and colorful displays of beautiful produce that I remembered, and exquisite handmade quilts and mouthwatering pies and cakes, and some of the handsomest livestock in the world. For lunch we had some of the best barbecue north of the Mason-Dixon Line, courtesy of the Ohio Pork Producer's Association, and yes, we did see the butter cow and have Swiss cheese sandwiches for supper.

Dinner from the Garden

FOR 6 TO 8

✍

MENU

Grilled Eggplant Steaks with
Just-Picked Tomato Sauce

Aunt Susie's Snap Beans
and Potatoes

Steamed Greens with
Garlic and Oil

Sweet Corn on the Cob

Swedish Beet Salad

• • •

Kitty Layne's Peach Dessert
with Cinnamon Ice Cream
(page 59)

When I moved back out of the city after twenty years, I quickly realized how much I had missed being out in the country every day. As much as I love the city, I don't think I ever stopped being a "farm boy," and once I got here I couldn't wait to get dirt under my fingernails. My acre is not quite the 604 acres my father farmed when I was growing up, but if I have even the slightest green tint to my thumb, I have to give Dad the credit. He's the old farmer who can make anything grow. Long before he ever farmed himself, he learned about growing things from his mother, who always kept a large kitchen garden and who once grew an apple and peach orchard from seeds. (To carry on the family tradition, I've just added two apple trees to the peach and cherry trees already on my property, so I've now got an orchard-to-be).

Dad's been retired from farming for years, but every year he still has a huge vegetable garden (which he maintains singlehandedly, even now) and a few fruit trees that annually supply most of the produce Dad puts up for use during the following winter and spring. My own little

Dad shows off an ear of his prize-winning
sweet corn (above left). His garden
(above) yields an abundance of produce.

vegetable patch is a postage stamp compared to Dad's kitchen garden, but I'm still just as proud of that first tomato as he is. So here's a dinner based on the best from the gardens, Dad's and mine.

Getting Ready Just about everything here should be as fresh as can be and cooked as close as possible to serving time. The ice cream can be made well in advance and so can the dessert; the beet salad and tomato sauce can be made early in the day, but everything else should be started only an hour or so before dinner.

First, pare the eggplant, then start the fire. Next, get the potatoes and beans started. Have the greens ready to be cooked and peel the corn. If you have an extra pair of hands available, have them grill the eggplant while the greens dish is tossed together and the corn is boiling.

Serve dinner with beer, lemonade, or iced tea.

Grilled Eggplant Steaks with Just-Picked Tomato Sauce

ॐ

SERVES 6 TO 8

Eggplant, being highly absorbent, takes on a wonderfully smoky flavor when it's cooked on the grill. The cool but highly seasoned fresh tomato sauce is a perfect partner. You might try grilling summer squash, sliced lengthwise, this way, too.

Sauce

3 medium very ripe tomatoes, peeled (see Note) and cut into ¼-inch dice
2 tablespoons olive oil
2 tablespoons chopped herbs (oregano, marjoram, thyme, basil, or a combination)
2 scallions, white and green parts, thinly sliced

⅛ teaspoon crushed red pepper flakes
¼ teaspoon salt

• • •

⅓ cup olive oil
2 garlic cloves, crushed
½ teaspoon freshly ground black pepper
1 large eggplant or 2 medium eggplants, peeled and cut into ⅜-inch-thick slices
Salt
¼ cup stone-ground yellow cornmeal, approximately
Tomato slices, for garnish

1. Make the sauce by combining all the ingredients in a bowl and mixing well. Cover and let stand at room temperature until serving. (*The sauce should be prepared no more than a few hours ahead of time.*)

2. In a small bowl, combine the olive oil, garlic, and pepper. Set aside.

3. Place the eggplant slices in a colander, sprinkling each slice lightly with salt. Place a small plate onto the eggplant to weigh it down slightly and allow the eggplant to drain for 30 minutes.

4. Prepare a charcoal fire. Soak hardwood chips in water for 30 minutes. When the coals are glowing and covered with gray ashes, scatter wood chips over the coals. When the chips begin smoking, the fire is ready.

5. Remove the eggplant slices from the colander and dry them with paper towels. Brush the eggplant lightly on both sides with the oil and dust them very lightly with cornmeal. Place the slices on a wax paper–lined platter, with wax paper between the layers.

6. Grill the eggplant about 3 inches above the coals until just tender and browned on both sides, about 5 minutes per side. Arrange the eggplant steaks on a platter, spoon some of the tomato sauce over them, and garnish with tomato slices. Serve additional sauce on the side.

Note: To peel tomatoes, drop them whole into boiling water for 1 minute. Remove them from the water, cool, and slip off the skins.

Aunt Susie's Snap Beans and Potatoes

SERVES 6 TO 8

My Great-Aunt Susie was an old-country cook who often flavored her vegetables with vinegar and bacon fat. Here's my somewhat lighter version of her potato and bean dish.

To fix the beans the traditional way, don't trim and halve them with a knife; snap them with your fingers.

- 4 medium potatoes, peeled and quartered
- ½ pound green beans, trimmed and halved
- ½ pound wax beans, trimmed and halved
- ¼ cup chopped smoked bacon (2 to 3 slices)
- 1 large onion, thinly sliced
- ¼ cup cider vinegar
- 2 teaspoons rosemary leaves *or* ½ teaspoon crumbled dried rosemary
- Pinch of sugar
- Salt and freshly ground black pepper

1. Put the potatoes in a pan with salted water to cover. Place the pan over high heat and boil the potatoes until barely tender, 15 to 20 minutes. Remove from the heat, rinse with cold water, and drain.

2. Meanwhile, put the beans in a separate pan with salted water to cover. Place over high heat and boil the beans for 5 minutes. Remove from the heat, rinse with cold water, and drain. Slice the potatoes and reserve.

3. In a large, heavy skillet over low heat, sauté the bacon until it renders some of its fat, 2 to 3 minutes. Add the onion and sauté until golden and tender, about 5 minutes. Add the vinegar and rosemary and stir to blend.

4. Add the beans and potatoes to the pan and cook, tossing occasionally, until the vegetables are heated through and coated with the skillet mixture, about 3 to 4 minutes. Season to taste with a pinch of sugar, salt, and pepper. Serve hot. *(The vegetables can be made early in the day; warm them by tossing in a skillet just before serving.)*

Fresh vegetables always taste best when they've just been picked and rushed onto the dinner table (opposite).

SWEET CORN ON THE COB

Everyone's got an opinion when it comes to how to cook "perfect" corn on the cob, but the truth is that the corn itself is the most important factor rather than the cooking method and timing. The fresher the corn, the better it will be. And if it's really fresh corn it doesn't need any butter, salt, or pepper. (By the way, "sweet corn" is what people eat; "field corn" is for the livestock.)

On our farm, the kettle would go onto the stove, and when the water was just beginning to bubble, one of us kids would be sent to the garden to pick the corn and husk it on the kitchen steps, then into the kettle it went. Now I don't grow corn in my garden, so I never have it quite that fresh anymore, but I do have a farm stand about a mile away.

When picking out corn, look for plump small kernels and light green husks; corn with large or slightly wrinkled kernels or dark green husks is often too old to be worth eating. Take the corn home and refrigerate it immediately. Here's how I cook it:

Place a large kettle of salted water over high heat and bring to a rolling boil. While the water is heating, husk the corn, reserving a few of the inner husks. Add the ears and the reserved husks, cover the kettle, and remove it from the heat; let stand 5 minutes. (The corn can stand for 10 minutes or so, staying hot and not overcooking.)

If corn is less than perfect, here are a few remedies: Old and tough corn may need to be boiled for 5 to 10 minutes to help tenderize it. If the corn was picked a day or so ago, the natural sugars have already begun turning to starch; a tablespoon of sugar added to the water will help sweeten it a little.

Steamed Greens with Garlic and Oil

❦

SERVES 6

Mustard greens and Swiss chard are greens that we all tend to forget about until we see big leafy bunches at a farm stand. If you've never had them and you come across them, give them a try. Spinach, which is more commonly available, is good cooked this way, too.

3 pounds greens (beet greens, mustard greens, spinach, or Swiss chard), washed well
3 tablespoons extra-virgin olive oil
1 tablespoon lemon juice
½ teaspoon dry mustard
1 garlic clove, finely chopped
Salt and freshly ground black pepper

1. If using mustard greens or spinach, place in a steamer basket over simmering water, cover, and steam until the leaves are wilted, about 5 minutes. Beet greens need a few minutes longer.

If using Swiss chard, cut the leaves from the ribs and diagonally cut the ribs into 1½-inch pieces. Place the ribs in a steamer basket over a pan of simmering water. Cover and steam the ribs until crisp-tender, about 10 minutes. Add the leaves and continue steaming until the leaves are tender, 3 to 5 minutes longer. Remove from the heat.

2. In a serving bowl, combine the oil, lemon juice, mustard, and garlic and whisk to blend. Season to taste with salt and pepper. Add the greens and toss well to coat with the oil mixture. Serve warm or at room temperature.

SUMMER GARDEN CHORES

- Weed the garden.
- Train the new growth on the climbing roses and prune them after the first bloom.
- Edge the drive, walkways, and flower beds.
- Keep everything well watered.
- Deadhead flowers after the blossoms die.
- Weed the garden.
- Mulch everything that needs it.
- Watch the roses for pests and disease.
- Mow the grass.
- Watch the lawn for crabgrass, ground ivy, and other undesirables.
- Chase away the deer!
- Feed the fruit trees, the vegetables, and roses.
- Weed the garden!

One of Dad's many garden chores is hanging freshly pulled onions to dry.

Swedish Beet Salad

❦

SERVES 6 TO 8

When I visited Stockholm a few years ago, I was a guest at several lavish smorgasbords, where beet salads always made an appearance. This version is especially refreshing on a warm summer evening.

¼ cup cider vinegar
½ cup sour cream
2 tablespoons sugar
1 tablespoon chopped dill
4 cups diced cooked beets (5 to 6, about 1 bunch)
2 carrots, cooked and diced
1 medium onion, thinly sliced

In a serving bowl, combine the vinegar, sour cream, sugar, and dill and whisk to blend. Add the beets, carrots, and onion and toss to coat the vegetables well with the dressing. Cover and refrigerate at least 2 hours before serving. *(Can made be up to a day before serving.)* Serve cold.

Beet Salad with Shrimp If you want to make the salad a bit more substantial to serve as a main course, add 1 cup cooked and peeled small shrimp and a handful of cooked peas. Serve mounded on a bed of leaf lettuce.

Kitty Layne's Peach Dessert

SERVES 10 TO 12

A favorite dessert at the Layne summer house at Rehoboth Beach, Delaware, this can be made in a matter of minutes. Kitty says she doesn't worry about the size of the egg; it just makes the dough more or less crumbly. She also uses anywhere from a cup to a cup and a half of granulated sugar in the dough. As you may have gathered, this is a rather informal recipe, but as Kitty says, "I don't worry much about the quantities of the ingredients. Usually it comes out okay, no matter what." And of course, now that I make Kitty's dessert with my own peaches, I think it comes out even better.

   7 cups sliced peaches
   1/3 cup firmly packed light brown sugar
   1 teaspoon ground cinnamon
   1 1/4 cups granulated sugar
   1 1/2 cups flour
   1 teaspoon baking powder
   2 eggs, lightly beaten
   1 teaspoon vanilla extract
   2 tablespoons butter

1. Preheat the oven to 350°F. Generously butter a 9 x 13-inch baking pan.

2. Distribute the sliced peaches evenly over the bottom of the pan. Sprinkle the brown sugar over the peaches and then sprinkle the cinnamon over the sugar.

3. In a mixing bowl, stir the granulated sugar, flour, and baking powder together with a fork, then stir in the eggs and vanilla to form a sticky, crumbly dough. Drop the dough by spoonfuls over the peaches, leaving spaces between for the juices to bubble up during baking, then dot with the butter.

4. Bake until nicely browned, about 35 minutes. Serve warm or at room temperature, topped with vanilla ice cream or whipped cream.

Kitty's cobblerlike fresh peach dessert.

An Afternoon Pie Social

❧

Mom's Rhubarb Custard Pie

My Favorite Elderberry Pie

Grandma Wynn's
Buttermilk Lemon Pie

Ken's Crazy Quilt
Red Raspberry Pie

Betty's Peaches and Cream Pie

My Nieces' Strawberry Tarts

Heather's Big Apple Pie

Iva Mae's Chocolate Angel Pie

Grandma Stapleton's
Spiced Carrot Pie

Jersey Plaid Pie

Pie is my favorite dessert. Sure, I like cakes, and cookies, and puddings, and so on, but you could take them all away as long as you leave me a wedge of warm, juicy pie.

Back home, pie socials were a major social event. Held in late summer, when the variety of fruits was at its peak, these were an excuse for home bakers to really show off, so that everyone could see just who really made the most golden and flakiest pie crust, and who could achieve the perfect balance of sweet and tart in an apple pie, and who could whip up the highest meringue.

The pie social was like any pot luck event, except there was even more food than usual: Every family would bring a covered dish and a pie. So you know we kids would do our best at out-eating one another. I have to admit that we Hadamuscin kids always held our own, probably because we got plenty of practice wolfing down Mom's pies at home.

For some reason, I don't have quite the same endurance I had a few decades ago, so in planning a pie social I'm willing to forgo the covered dishes and cut to the chase.

Serve as many different pies as you'd like (each pie yields 8 good-sized slices) and have plenty of lemonade and iced coffee.

Getting Ready Obviously, no one person is going to make all these pies at once (though two of us did make them all in a day for the photographs). It only takes a few minutes to make any of the pastry doughs here, but they can be made a day in advance, wrapped well, and stored in the refrigerator. Or make the pastry up to a few weeks in advance and freeze it; thaw in the refrigerator before using.

Some fruit fillings can be prepared a few

Our pie buffet is set out in the garden on a table covered with 1950s printed tablecloths.

hours in advance, but any fruits that brown easily, such as apples and peaches, should be pared just before baking time. Fruit pies are best made on the day they are served so the bottom crusts don't become soggy. (But there's nothing wrong with a slice of leftover fruit pie for breakfast!)

Basic Pastry

✌

MAKES 1 CRUST FOR A 9-INCH PIE

Years ago, Mom always used lard as the shortening in her pie crusts; we butchered our own pigs, so there was always plenty available. Nowadays Mom uses a combination of vegetable shortening and butter for the best texture and flavor, and hers is the recipe I always use. Mom always uses her fingers for cutting in the fats, but my hands are too hot, so I use a pastry blender. (Pastry can be made with the food processor, but it's never as flaky or tender as pastry made the old-fashioned way.)

1½ cups all-purpose flour
Scant ½ teaspoon salt
1½ teaspoons sugar
¼ cup vegetable shortening, chilled
¼ cup (½ stick) cold butter
3 to 4 tablespoons ice water

1. In a large mixing bowl, sift together the flour, salt, and sugar. Using your fingertips, rub the fats into the dry ingredients until coarse and crumbly in texture. Do this quickly to keep the fats cold and solid, and do not overwork. (Or use a pastry blender to combine the dry ingredients and the shortenings.)

2. Starting with 3 tablespoonfuls, add the water and work it into the flour-shortening mixture to form a ball of dough. Add 1 or 2 more tablespoons of water if necessary to hold the dough together. Wrap the dough ball in wax paper and chill for 1 hour before using.

Orange Pastry Double the sugar, substitute orange juice for the water, and add the grated rind of a small orange.

Cream Cheese Pastry

❧

MAKES 1 CRUST FOR A 9-INCH PIE

1 3-ounce package cream cheese, softened
½ cup (1 stick) butter, softened
2 tablespoons milk
2 cups plus 2 tablespoons all-purpose
  flour

In a mixing bowl, cream the cheese and butter together until well blended, then beat in the milk. Add the flour in thirds, mixing well after each addition. Form the dough into a ball, wrap in wax paper, and chill for 1 hour before using.

Mom's Rhubarb Custard Pie

❧

MAKES ONE 9-INCH PIE

I've always got a few bags of rhubarb in the freezer so I can make this old-fashioned pie anytime I've a yen for it. (If using frozen rhubarb, allow it to thaw and drain in a colander before using it in the filling.)

Double recipe Orange Pastry (page 85)
3 large eggs
2 cups sugar
3 tablespoons milk
¼ cup all-purpose flour
½ teaspoon nutmeg
4 cups diced rhubarb
2 tablespoons sugar mixed with
  ½ teaspoon ground cinnamon

1. Preheat the oven to 400°F. Divide the pastry in half; roll out 1 portion and use it to line a 9-inch pie pan.

2. In a mixing bowl, combine the eggs, 2 cups sugar, milk, flour, and nutmeg and beat until smooth, then stir in the rhubarb. Pour the mixture into the prepared pie pan.

3. Roll out the remaining pastry and cut slits in the center to allow steam to escape during baking. Carefully cover the filling with it. Trim, seal,

and crimp the edges. Brush the crust with milk and sprinkle with sugar and cinnamon.

4. Bake until the custard is set and the crust is a deep golden brown, 40 to 45 minutes. Transfer the pie to a wire rack to cool. Serve slightly warm or at room temperature. If making ahead, store the pie in the refrigerator.

My Favorite Elderberry Pie

❧

MAKES ONE 9-INCH PIE

My very favorite pie of all. When I was a kid I used to gather the wild elderberries from bushes along country roadsides and fencerows in the pastures. Now, I've got a deal with my publisher, Michelle Sidrane: She brings me elderberries from the countryside near her house in upstate New York and she gets a pie in return.

1¼ cups sugar
⅓ cup all-purpose flour
7 cups elderberries
Juice of 1 lemon
Double recipe Cream Cheese Pastry
  (above)
2 tablespoons butter

1. In a mixing bowl, stir together the sugar and flour. Add the elderberries and toss welll; add the lemon juice and toss again. Let stand 15 minutes.

2. Preheat the oven to 400°F.

3. Divide the pastry in half and roll out two circles. Use one circle to line a 9-inch pie pan. Fill the crust with the elderberry mixture and dot with the butter. Use the remaining pastry to cover the filling and trim, seal, and crimp the edges.

4. Bake the pie for 10 minutes, then reduce the heat to 350°F. Bake until the filling is bubbly and the crust is nicely browned, 35 to 40 minutes. Cool on a wire rack and serve warm or at room temperature.

Grandma Wynn's Buttermilk Lemon Pie

MAKES ONE 9-INCH PIE

When my grandmother worked as a cook in a restaurant years ago, this custardy pie was a favorite of the customers. It's long been a family favorite, too.

Basic Pastry (page 85)
1 cup sugar
3 tablespoons flour
½ teaspoon salt
¼ cup (½ stick) butter, melted and cooled
2 cups buttermilk
4 large eggs
1 teaspoon vanilla extract
Juice and grated rind of 1 lemon
Dash of nutmeg
Lemon slices for garnish

1. Preheat the oven to 400°F. Roll out the pastry and use it to line a 9-inch pie pan, then crimp the edge.

2. In a mixing bowl, combine the sugar, flour, and salt. Add the butter, buttermilk, eggs, vanilla, and lemon juice and rind and beat until the mixture is smooth.

3. Pour the mixture into the pie pan and sprinkle lightly with nutmeg. Bake for 10 minutes. Reduce the heat to 325°F. and bake until the custard is set and golden brown, 25 to 30 minutes. Cool the pie on a wire rack and chill. Serve cold, garnished with lemon slices.

My grandmother's golden buttermilk pie has always been a year-round family favorite.

"Haphazard" strips of golden pastry add to the beauty of this juicy raspberry pie.

Ken's Crazy Quilt Red Raspberry Pie

MAKES ONE 9-INCH PIE

Next to elderberry pie, I like raspberry pie best. This pie has an irregular lattice top, resembling the pattern of a crazy quilt, hence the name. The recipe can be varied using red or black raspberries or blackberries.

1 cup sugar
3 tablespoons cornstarch
¼ teaspoon salt
6 cups red raspberries (see Note)
3 tablespoons butter
2 tablespoons flour
Double recipe Basic Pastry (page 85)
1 large egg yolk, lightly beaten
    with 1 tablespoon milk
Sugar, for sprinkling

1. In a medium, heavy saucepan, combine the sugar, cornstarch, and salt and mix well. Add the raspberries and toss to coat with the sugar mixture. Place the pan over medium heat and cook, stirring often to prevent sticking (the berries will break up, but that's okay), until the mixture is bubbly and thickened, about 7 minutes. Stir in the butter and remove from the heat. Sprinkle the flour over the berry mixture and stir it in. Allow the mixture to cool.

2. Preheat the oven to 400°F. Divide the pastry in half and roll one half out into a ⅛-inch-thick circle. Line a 9-inch pie pan with the pastry circle. Roll out the remaining pastry.

3. Fill the lined pie pan with the berry mixture, then, using the remaining pastry, top with an irregular lattice top (see photograph above). Trim, seal, and crimp the edges. Carefully brush the pastry with the beaten egg yolk mixture and sprinkle generously with sugar.

4. Bake for 15 minutes, reduce the heat to 350°F., and continue baking until the crust is nicely browned, about 30 minutes longer. Transfer the pie to a wire rack to cool and serve warm or at room temperature.

Note: Thawed frozen berries, well drained, can be substituted for fresh ones if necessary.

An old pie basket holds two peach pies decorated with peach leaves.

Betty's Peaches and Cream Pie

MAKES ONE 9-INCH PIE

Some store-bought versions have given cream cheese pies a bad reputation. They're usually made up of overly sweet fillings topped with a brightly colored goo that doesn't taste much like anything but sugar. My sister Betty's pie, on the other hand, has a thin layer of cream cheese filling, lots of fresh peaches, and a glossy glaze.

Basic Pastry (page 85)
2 3-ounce packages cream cheese, softened
2 tablespoons milk
1 teaspoon grated lemon rind
3 tablespoons confectioners' sugar
⅛ teaspoon salt
½ teaspoon vanilla extract
1 cup chopped peaches
⅔ cup granulated sugar
1 tablespoon lemon juice
1 tablespoon water
5 cups sliced peaches

1. Preheat the oven to 425°F. Line a 9-inch pie pan with the pastry, prick well with a fork, and crimp the edges. Fill the pan halfway with dry beans (I reuse the same beans for this purpose) and bake until the pastry is nicely browned, about 15 minutes. Remove the pan to a wire rack. When cool, remove the weights.

2. In a mixing bowl, combine the cream cheese, milk, lemon rind, confectioners' sugar, salt, and vanilla and mix well with a fork. Spread this mixture evenly over the bottom of the baked pie shell and chill until set, about 1 hour.

3. Meanwhile, in a medium, heavy saucepan, combine the chopped peaches, the granulated sugar, lemon juice, and water. Place over low heat and cook, stirring constantly and crushing the peaches against the side of the pan with the back of the spoon, until the mixture is thick and syrupy, about 10 minutes. Cool to lukewarm.

4. Arrange the sliced peaches, overlapping them, over the cheese mixture. With a spoon, drizzle the cooked mixture over the sliced peaches, covering them completely to prevent browning. Chill the pie until serving, at least 2 hours.

Simple tarts of glazed berries and custard.

My Nieces' Strawberry Tarts

ℰ

MAKES TEN 4-INCH TARTS

When my nieces Monica and Cathy were younger these little red tarts made them feel very grown up and elegant.

Custard

1 cup milk

¼ cup sugar

3 tablespoons flour

1/4 teaspoon salt

4 large egg yolks, lightly beaten

2 teaspoons almond extract

2 tablespoons (¼ stick) butter, softened

• • •

Double recipe Orange Pastry (page 85)

1 pint strawberries, hulled and thinly sliced

½ cup currant jelly, melted and cooled

1. To make the custard, heat the milk in the top of a double boiler over simmering water until just below the boiling point. In a mixing bowl,

combine the sugar, flour, and salt and mix well. Gradually whisk the hot milk into the dry ingredients. Pour the mixture back into the top of the double boiler and cook, whisking constantly, until the mixture comes to a boil and is quite thick and smooth.

2. Remove the pan from the heat and, one at a time, whisk in the egg yolks. Return to the heat and continue cooking for 1 minute longer. Remove from the heat and whisk for 2 minutes to cool slightly. Whisk in the almond extract and butter until smooth, then allow the mixture to cool, then chill in the refrigerator.

3. Preheat the oven to 375°F. Roll out the pastry and use it to line ten 4-inch tart pans, then prick the pastry all over with a fork. Bake the pastry until golden brown, 15 to 20 minutes, then remove the pans to wire racks to allow the tart shells to cool.

TIPS FOR MAKING FRUIT PIES

• Fruit shrinks when it's cooked; raw fruit should be mounded slightly above the height of the rim of the pan so the baked pie doesn't end up with a sunken center. Adjust the quantity of fruit and other filling ingredients if necessary.

• Bake a pie as soon as it's filled so the juices don't make the crust soggy.

• Not every 9-inch pie pan has the same depth or capacity; the quantities here are for a standard ovenproof glass (Pyrex) 9-inch pan. Adjust the quantity of filling to the pan being used.

• Fruit pies not only bubble up but tend to bubble over while they're baking, so it's a good idea to place a foil-lined baking sheet on the bottom shelf of the oven to keep the oven floor clean.

• If the raw fruit being used seems especially juicy, add a few teaspoons more thickener (flour or cornstarch, as the recipe indicates). If the fruit seems to be lacking in flavor, an extra squeeze of lemon juice or orange juice will help perk it up.

4. Fill the tart shells halfway with custard, then arrange overlapping strawberry slices over the custard, covering it completely. Brush the berries with currant jelly, covering the surface to the edges of the pastry. Store the tarts in the refrigerator until ready to serve.

Heather's Big Apple Pie

MAKES ONE LARGE PIE

Mom recently taught my niece Heather to make pie crust and Heather's been baking pies like crazy ever since. This open-faced, streusel-topped apple pie is a favorite of her new husband Rob.

Double recipe Basic Pastry (page 85)
½ cup sugar
1 teaspoon ground cinnamon
2 tablespoons flour
6 cups sliced baking apples (Heather uses a combination of MacIntosh and Granny Smith)

Topping
3 tablespoons butter, softened
¼ cup sugar
1 teaspoon ground cinnamon
¾ cup all-purpose flour
½ cup coarsely chopped walnuts

1. On a floured surface, roll out the dough to a circle about ³⁄₁₆-inch thick. Carefully transfer the dough circle to an ungreased baking sheet.

2. In a mixing bowl, combine the sugar, cinnamon, and flour. Add the apples and toss well. Mound the apple slices evenly over the dough, leaving about 1½ inches dough uncovered around the edge.

3. Preheat the oven to 450°F.

4. Make the topping by combining all the ingredients and mixing with your fingers until crumbly. Sprinkle the topping over the apples. Turn the uncovered dough up over the filling, making pleats every 2 inches or so (this doesn't

A rustic version of everyone's favorite pie.

need to be done perfectly; the pie should have a rustic appearance).

5. Bake the pie 10 minutes, then turn the heat down to 350°F. Continue baking until the apples are tender and the crust is golden brown, 30 to 35 minutes. Serve warm or at room temperature.

GLAZING PASTRY

Pastry doesn't need to be glazed, but I usually like to enhance the appearance of a baked pie, to gild the lily, so to speak. Brushing unbaked pastry lightly with milk will help the baked crust have a rich and even brown color. For a golden glossy baked crust, brush an unbaked crust with a mixture of 1 egg lightly beaten with 1 tablespoon milk. Either of these two glazes can be sprinkled with sugar to add a little sparkle to the baked pie. Pies can also be left unglazed and lightly dusted with confectioners' sugar just before serving. In the recipes I've included the method of glazing used on the pies pictured here, but it's really up to the baker.

Iva Mae's Chocolate Angel Pie

৵

MAKES ONE 9-INCH PIE

Baked meringue pie shells almost always crack and collapse in the center, but don't worry about it—once the pie is filled, no one will ever know. Remember that meringues can be a bit temperamental, so this pie should only be made on a dry, not-too-hot day. (If the weather's uncooperative and you still have a craving for chocolate, try the fudge pie on page 151.)

Meringue Shell
4 large egg whites
⅛ teaspoon salt
¼ teaspoon cream of tartar
1 cup sugar
½ teaspoon almond extract
½ cup finely chopped almonds, lightly
  toasted

Chocolate Filling
8 large egg yolks
1 cup sugar
1 cup milk
4 ounces semisweet chocolate, melted and
  cooled
1½ teaspoons vanilla extract
½ pint raspberries
½ pint heavy cream, whipped

1. Preheat the oven to 275°F. Lightly grease a 9-inch nonmetallic pie pan.

2. In the bowl of an electric mixer, combine the egg whites, salt, and cream of tartar and beat until soft peaks form. Gradually beat in 1 cup sugar, beating until shiny, somewhat stiff peaks form, then beat in the almond extract. Fold in the almonds.

3. Spread this mixture evenly in the pie shell, lining the bottom and mounding up at the sides. Bake until lightly browned, about 1 hour. Turn off the oven, open the door, and allow the crust to cool.

4. Meanwhile, make the chocolate filling. In the

electric mixer bowl, beat the egg yolks until they are thick and lemon-colored. Slowly beat in the sugar, then beat in the milk and melted chocolate. Transfer the mixture to the top of a double boiler over simmering water or a heavy saucepan over low heat.

5. Cook, stirring constantly, until the mixture thickens, about 10 minutes. Remove the pan from the heat and continue to stir for a minute, then stir in the vanilla. Allow the mixture to cool.

6. Spoon the cooled filling into the cooled pie shell. Refrigerate until serving. Just before serving, garnish the pie with the raspberries and dabs of whipped cream.

Grandma Stapleton's Spiced Carrot Pie

৵

MAKES ONE 9-INCH PIE

Carrot pies, similar to pumpkin pies, were not at all unusual a few generations ago. And you don't have to wait for pumpkin season to come along—carrot pies can be made all year long with fresh carrots.

Cream Cheese Pastry (page 86)
1½ cups mashed cooked carrots
3 large eggs
1½ cups light cream
½ cup firmly packed light brown sugar
½ cup granulated sugar
½ teaspoon salt
Grated rind of 1 small orange
1 teaspoon ground cinnamon
1 teaspoon ground ginger
¼ teaspoon grated nutmeg
¼ teaspoon ground cloves

1. Preheat the oven to 400°F. Line a 9-inch pie pan with the pastry.

2. Combine the remaining ingredients in a mixing bowl and beat until smooth and well blended. Pour the filling into the lined pie pan and bake until a knife inserted in the center comes out clean, about 1 hour. (If the crust begins to

An unusual combination of blueberries and cranberries make an especially tasty pie.

get too brown, cover the edges of the pie with strips of aluminum foil.)

3. Cool the pie on a wire rack and chill before serving.

Orange-Glazed Carrot Pie Melt ½ cup fine-cut Seville orange marmalade in a small, heavy saucepan over low heat. Spread the marmalade over the surface of the cooled pie and allow to cool before chilling.

Jersey Plaid Pie

℘

MAKES ONE 9-INCH PIE

Blueberries and cranberries, both big crops here in New Jersey, are combined in this colorful lattice-topped pie. They're not really in season at the same time, but both berries freeze well, so you can have this pie any time at all.

Double recipe Basic Pastry (page 85)
4 cups (2 pints) blueberries
3 cups (1 12-ounce bag) cranberries

⅓ cup all-purpose flour
1¼ cups sugar
½ teaspoon ground cinnamon
¼ teaspoon ground cloves
¼ teaspoon ground ginger
2 tablespoons orange juice
1 large egg, lightly beaten with
    1 tablespoon milk

1. Preheat the oven to 400°F. Divide the pastry in half; roll out one portion and use it to line a 9-inch pie pan.

2. In a mixing bowl, combine the berries, flour, sugar, spices, and orange juice and mix well. Transfer this mixture into the prepared pie pan. Use the remaining pastry to make a lattice top. Trim, seal, and crimp the edges. Lightly brush the pastry with the beaten egg mixture.

3. Bake for 15 minutes, reduce the heat to 350°F., and continue baking until the filling is bubbly and the crust is a deep golden brown, 20 to 25 minutes. Transfer the pie to a wire rack to cool and serve warm or at room temperature.

Putting Things By

ℒℴ

Spiced Cantaloupe Pickle

Freezer Corn Relish

Spiced Pumpkin Butter

Pumpkin Puree

Pickled Baby Beets

Patchwork Vegetable Pickles

Hot Jerusalem Artichoke Pickle

Spiced Pickled Lady Apples

Apple Ketchup

Squash and Pear Chutney

"Hot-as-Hades" Pepper Jam

Pink Applesauce

Mom's Summer Chow Chow

Cranberry Dessert Wine

On our farm, canning was a huge production. Various items were put up sporadically throughout the summer, but in September, things really geared up for a month-long canning marathon. Produce was picked early in the morning, then sent up to the house. Behind the kitchen, there was a huge workroom/storeroom where we kids were put to work, shucking sweet corn, snapping beans, skinning peaches and tomatoes, bundling herbs to be dried, cleaning jars, and so on. As we completed each task, the produce was passed into the kitchen, where Mom and her helper had huge kettles steaming away. Sometimes there were so many jars and bushel baskets piled up all over the big kitchen that you couldn't see the countertops or the floor. And when we were all finished, there would be hundreds and hundreds of jars—vegetables, fruits, pickles, relishes, and jellies and jams—stacked in neat rows on the shelves in the cellar.

Back then, we did all this canning because this was our food supply for the fall and the winter. Now, when this production goes on in my kitchen, it's because I want to have a few homemade "extras" on hand, so the production is on a much smaller scale. Everything here is used in menus throughout the book, and everything makes great homemade gifts, as well.

A weekend project in the kitchen can yield rows and rows of good things to make fall and winter meals even better (opposite).

A FEW NOTES ON CANNING

• Inspect all produce carefully; fruits and vegetables should be at their peak, not beyond it. If any signs of bruising or spoilage exist, cut them away completely.

• Always wash canning jars and lids well and sterilize them by boiling for 15 minutes just before using.

• To be absolutely certain that no spoilage will occur after canning, process all pickles and relishes in a hot-water bath. To do this, place sealed jars at least an inch apart on a rack in a large kettle. Pour warm water into the kettle to cover the jars by 2 inches and gradually bring the water to a boil. Boil half-pint jars for 10 minutes, pint jars for 15 minutes, and quart jars for 20 minutes. Remove the jars with tongs and allow to cool gradually before labeling and storing.

• When opening any home-canned jar, if there is any reason to think that spoilage has occurred, discard the contents.

Spiced Cantaloupe Pickle

ℰ

MAKES ABOUT 3 PINTS

A variation on the more usual watermelon rind pickle, this is especially good with ham. Cantaloupe is usually sold slightly underripe, so when you buy it it's ready for pickling.

    2 medium, slightly underripe cantaloupes
    4 cups (1 quart) white vinegar
    2 cups apple juice
    1 tablespoon whole cloves
    1 tablespoon grated gingerroot *or*
        1 teaspoon ground ginger
    3 cinnamon sticks
    4 cups sugar

1. Quarter the cantaloupe and remove the seeds. Cut the melon into ¾-inch chunks, being careful not to include any of the green rind. Place

the cantaloupe in a heatproof, nonreactive bowl. Reserve.

2. Combine the vinegar, apple juice, and spices in a nonreactive pan. Place over medium-high heat and bring to a boil. Then stir in the sugar until dissolved. Reduce the heat to low and simmer for 30 minutes. Add the cantaloupe and simmer until the melon is translucent, about 20 minutes, then remove the pan from the heat.

3. Using a slotted spoon, carefully spoon the melon into sterilized 1-pint jars. Pour the liquid through a small sieve over the cantaloupe, covering it completely and leaving ¼-inch headspace. Seal the jars.

4. Process the jars in a boiling-water bath (left) for 15 minutes. Allow the jars to cool, dry and label them, and store in a cool dark place. Refrigerate the pickle after opening.

Freezer Corn Relish

ℰ

MAKES ABOUT 3 PINTS

When corn is plentiful and inexpensive, I make a few batches of this easy relish to store away for later on in the year. I like the relish so well that I often use it in more than the usual ways, such as in the muffins on page 75 or even as a salad, atop a bed of leaf lettuce and chunks of tomato.

    2 medium red onions, chopped
    1 large green bell pepper, seeded and
        chopped
    1 large red bell pepper, seeded and
        chopped
    5 cups freshly scraped corn kernels
        (see Note)
    1½ cups sugar
    1 teaspoon salt
    1 teaspoon celery seeds
    ½ teaspoon ground turmeric
    ½ teaspoon crushed hot red pepper flakes
    1½ cups cider vinegar
    ½ cup corn oil

In a medium, heavy saucepan, combine all the ingredients. Place over medium-high heat and bring the mixture to a boil. Reduce the heat and simmer, uncovered, stirring occasionally, for 20 minutes. Transfer the relish to 1-pint containers, cover tightly, and freeze. Allow to thaw in the refrigerator for 24 hours before using.

Note: Out of season, thawed frozen corn kernels can be substituted for fresh; add them during the last 10 minutes of cooking.

Spiced Pumpkin Butter

ℬ

MAKES ABOUT 3 HALF-PINTS

This thick, spicy butter can be used anywhere you'd use apple butter, such as on hot buttered biscuits or toasted English muffins. One of my favorite ways of having it is spread over cream cheese on black bread or nut bread.

   3 cups Pumpkin Puree (recipe follows)
     or 1 29-ounce can pumpkin
   ¾ cup apple cider
   1¼ cups firmly packed light brown sugar
   1 teaspoon ground cinnamon
   1 teaspoon ground ginger
   ¼ teaspoon ground cloves
   ¼ teaspoon grated nutmeg

1. Preheat the oven to 275°F. Combine all the ingredients in a heavy 2-quart baking dish and mix well. Cover the baking dish loosely with its lid or with aluminum foil. Bake, stirring occasionally, until the mixture is darkened and quite thick, about 1½ to 2 hours.

2. Spoon the mixture into half-pint jars, leaving ¼-inch headspace. Seal the jars and process in a boiling-water bath for 10 minutes. Allow the jars to cool, dry and label them, and store in a cool dark place. Refrigerate the butter after opening.

Pumpkin butter, instead of the more usual apple butter, is a nice surprise — and it couldn't be easier to make.

Pumpkin Puree

ℬ

I make enough of this to freeze to get me through the holidays; remember that it takes 1½ to 2 cups puree (depending on the recipe used) to make a pumpkin pie and 3 cups to make Spiced Pumpkin Butter (preceding recipe).

1. Cut the top and bottom from a medium sugar pumpkin (3 to 5 pounds), then cut off the skin as if peeling a very large apple. Cut the pumpkin into quarters, scoop out the seeds, then cut the pumpkin into 1-inch chunks.

2. Place the cubes in a large pan and cover with salted water by 2 inches. Place the pan over medium-high heat and bring to a boil. Boil the pumpkin until very tender, about 12 minutes. Drain in a colander.

3. Place the pumpkin in a large bowl. Mash with a potato masher, then beat with a wooden spoon until smooth. Allow the puree to cool, then pack into freezer bags and freeze.

Almost any crisp and colorful vegetable can be added to Patchwork Vegetable Pickles.

Pickled Baby Beets

ℰ

MAKES 4 PINTS

6 cups white vinegar
2 cups sugar
1 teaspoon salt
1 teaspoon ground ginger
2 teaspoons whole cloves
½ teaspoon caraway seeds
4 pounds very small beets, cooked and
  peeled (see Note)
2 small onions, thinly sliced and separated
  into rings

1. In a medium, heavy saucepan, combine the vinegar, sugar, salt, spices, and caraway seeds. Over medium-low heat, bring the mixture to a simmer and simmer 5 minutes.

2. Meanwhile, layer the beets and onion rings into 4 sterilized pint jars. Pour the hot vinegar mixture into the jars, covering the vegetables completely and leaving ¼-inch headspace. Seal the jars and process them in a boiling-water bath (page 96) for 15 minutes. Cool, dry and label the jars, then store them in a cool place.

Note: Beets can be roasted in a 350°F. oven until tender; when cool enough to handle, the skins will slip off easily. If very small beets are unavailable, use larger beets and halve or quarter them after peeling.

Patchwork Vegetable Pickles

ℰ

MAKES 6 TO 7 PINTS

Mixed pickles came about when farm women came to the end of their canning chores and had just little bits of a few things left but not enough of anything for a batch of a single kind of pickle. So they combined vegetables and each jar ended up with a multicolored patchwork appearance. The vegetables can be varied according to what's available, but the result is always more than the sum of its parts.

3½ cups cider vinegar
¼ cup salt
3 cups sugar
½ teaspoon dry mustard
1 tablespoon mustard seeds

1 tablespoon celery seeds

1 teaspoon whole cloves

1 teaspoon black peppercorns

1½ pound Kirby cucumbers, cut into
½-inch slices

1 pound tiny white onions (1 to 2 inches
long)

1 10-ounce box Brussels sprouts, washed
well and halved

½ pound carrots, peeled and cut into
¼-inch slices

2 large red bell peppers, cored, seeded,
and cut into 1-inch triangles

2 celery stalks, diagonally cut into
½-inch slices

1. In a large kettle, combine the vinegar, salt, sugar, dry mustard, mustard seeds, celery seeds, cloves, and peppercorns. Place over medium heat and bring to a boil, stirring to dissolve the sugar and salt.

2. Add the vegetables to the pan and let the liquid come to a boil again, then remove from the heat. With a slotted spoon, transfer the vegetables to sterilized pint jars. Spoon the liquid over the vegetables, leaving ¼-inch headspace. Seal the jars and process them in a boiling-water bath (page 96) for 10 minutes. Cool, dry and label the jars, then store in a cool place.

Hot Jerusalem Artichoke Pickle

ℐℴ

MAKES ABOUT 4 PINTS

Jerusalem artichokes, also known as sunchokes, are crisp and mildly flavored, perfect for making spicy pickles.

4 cups white wine vinegar

1 cup firmly packed light brown sugar

2 pounds Jerusalem artichokes

Juice of 1 lemon

1 medium onion, thinly sliced

4 large garlic cloves, peeled

4 small whole hot peppers, such as
jalapeño

1. In a heavy saucepan over medium heat, combine the vinegar and brown sugar. Bring to a boil, reduce the heat to low, and simmer 5 minutes.

2. Meanwhile, peel the chokes, cut them into ½-inch chunks, and toss them with the lemon juice. Layer the chokes and onion into sterilized pint jars. Add a garlic clove and hot pepper to each jar.

3. Pour the simmering liquid over the vegetables, leaving ¼-inch headspace. Seal the jars and process them in a boiling-water bath (page 96) for 10 minutes. Cool, dry and label the jars , and store in a cool place.

Spiced Pickled Lady Apples

ℐℴ

MAKES ABOUT 3 QUARTS

Lady apples are small and pretty and perfect for pickling. They used to be available only at orchard farm stands and farmers' markets, but this fall I found them at my local supermarket. If you can't find lady apples, crab apples can be substituted.

4 cups sugar

3 cups cider vinegar

1 cup cranberry juice cocktail

2 3- to 4-inch cinnamon sticks, broken
in half

2 teaspoons whole cloves

4 pounds lady apples, washed well

1. In a large, nonreactive saucepan, combine the sugar, vinegar, cranberry juice cocktail, and spices. Place over medium-high heat, bring to a boil, and boil 10 minutes, uncovered.

2. Carefully pack the apples into sterilized 1-pint jars, then spoon the liquid over them. Seal the jars, leaving ¼-inch headspace. Process the jars in a boiling-water bath (page 96) for 10 minutes. Cool, dry and label the jars, and store in a cool place. Let stand 3 weeks before using.

Apple Ketchup

୫

MAKES ABOUT 2 PINTS

Years ago, ketchup did not necessarily mean tomato; different varieties were made from all kinds of fruits, nuts, and even mushrooms. Here's a spicy apple ketchup that goes well with grilled or roasted pork, veal, and fowl, and with "City Chicken" (page 159).

    10 tart apples, peeled, cored, and coarsely
       chopped
    2 cups apple cider
    2 cups cider vinegar
    2 cups firmly packed light brown sugar
    3 medium onions, chopped
    3 large garlic cloves, chopped
    2 tablespoons chopped gingerroot
    1 teaspoon salt
    1 teaspoon ground cinnamon
    1 teaspoon ground cloves
    1 teaspoon dry mustard
    ½ teaspoon finely ground black pepper
    ½ teaspoon ground cayenne pepper

1. In a large, heavy saucepan, combine all the ingredients, then place over medium-high heat. Bring to a boil, reduce the heat to low, and simmer, stirring frequently to prevent sticking, until the apples are mushy and the mixture is quite thick, about 1 hour. Remove from the heat.

2. In batches, transfer the mixture to the bowl of a food processor fitted with the steel chopping blade and puree until smooth. Transfer to sterilized pint jars and seal. Process in a boiling-water bath (page 96) for 10 minutes. Cool, dry and label the jars, and store in a cool place.

Squash and Pear Chutney

୫

MAKES ABOUT 7 HALF-PINTS

    1 medium butternut squash (about 2½
       pounds), peeled, seeded, and cut into
       ½-inch chunks
    2 medium onions, coarsely chopped
    2 large garlic cloves, thinly sliced
    ½ cup granulated sugar
    1 cup firmly packed light brown sugar
    2 teaspoons salt
    2 teaspoons ground ginger
    1 teaspoon dry mustard
    1 teaspoon ground cinnamon
    ½ teaspoon ground cloves
    ¼ teaspoon ground cayenne
    1½ cups red wine vinegar
    5 Anjou or Bosc pears, peeled, cored,
       and cut into ½-inch chunks

1. In a large, heavy, nonreactive saucepan, combine the squash, onions, garlic, sugars, salt, spices, and vinegar. Place over medium-high heat and bring to a boil. Reduce the heat to low and simmer, uncovered, stirring occasionally until the squash is just tender, about 45 minutes. Add the pears and simmer until the pears are tender, about 15 minutes longer.

2. In batches, transfer the mixture to the bowl of a food processor fitted with the steel chopping blade. Pulse a few times to break up the squash and pears. If the mixture seems a little thin, return it to the pan and cook down for a few more minutes.

3. Transfer the mixture to sterilized half-pint jars, seal, and process in a boiling-water bath (page 96) for 10 minutes. Cool, dry and label the jars, then store in a cool place.

"Hot-as-Hades" Pepper Jam

୫

MAKES ABOUT 6 HALF-PINTS

The classic way to serve hot pepper jam is on crackers spread with cream cheese, but I use it in other ways, too: for glazing a ham, as a condiment for grilled chicken or swordfish, and on ham or smoked turkey sandwiches.

I make the jam using different color combinations of bell peppers—red and yellow for fall and mostly red with a little green and yellow for Christmastime. Some people use a few drops of food coloring to "enhance" the color, but it always looks phony to me. You can cut down on the hot peppers if you like, and don't forget to wear rubber gloves and eye protection when chopping them; they burn. The peppers and garlic can be finely chopped in a food processor, but be careful not to let them turn to mush.

1¾ cups very finely chopped bell peppers (any color or a combination)
4 or 5 small, hot peppers, such as jalapeños, very finely chopped
1 small garlic clove, very finely chopped
6½ cups sugar
1½ cups cider vinegar
1 6-ounce bottle or 2 3-ounce packets liquid pectin

In a large, heavy saucepan, combine the peppers, garlic, sugar, and vinegar and place over

"Hot-as-Hades" Pepper Jam should be made as hot as you can stand it!

high heat. Bring the mixture to a boil and add the pectin. Bring the mixture to a boil again, then quickly transfer to hot sterilized half-pint jars and seal. Store the jars in a cool place.

Pink Applesauce

MAKES ABOUT 2 PINTS

My grandmother used to make big batches of applesauce every fall, and as a small child I was always fascinated at how the result was always a slightly different hue, depending on the colorings of the skins. To ensure that I always have a rosy pink sauce, I pick the reddest apples I can find and I "cheat" just a little by using cranberry juice instead of water (adding a little interest to the flavor, as well).

Homemade applesauce is delicious for breakfast with a dollop of yogurt, and it becomes one of the most wonderful snacks in the world atop warm gingerbread. Make a double or triple batch and can or freeze the extra sauce.

8 tart red cooking apples, such as Rome Beauties, quartered and cored (do not peel)
1½ cups cranberry juice cocktail
2 tablespoons sugar
Juice of 1 lemon

1. Combine all the ingredients in a medium, nonreactive saucepan, place over medium-high heat, and bring to a boil. Reduce the heat, cover the pan loosely, and simmer until the apples are very mushy, about 30 minutes. Remove from the heat and cool slightly.

2. Using a Foley mill, strain the applesauce (or strain by pushing the mixture through a coarse sieve with the back of a spoon). Discard the skins left in the mill (or sieve). Transfer the applesauce to a small bowl, cover tightly, and chill until serving. Or transfer to sterilized pint jars, seal, and process in a boiling-water bath (page 96) for 15 minutes. Cool and label the jars, then store in a cool place.

Mom's Summer Chow Chow

MAKES ABOUT 4 PINTS

I like this sweet-and-sour mustard-sauced concoction, a cross between a pickle and a relish, with ham, grilled chicken, or thin slices of cold roast beef. The vegetables used can be mixed and matched according to availability at the market; for example, if green tomatoes are unavailable, substitute additional cauliflower and/or cucumbers.

3 cups cauliflower flowerets
2 cups peeled pearl onions

2 cups coarsely chopped green tomatoes
2 large green bell peppers, coarsely chopped
2 large red bell peppers, coarsely chopped
6 Kirby or other small cucumbers, cut into ¼-inch slices
3 tablespoons salt
2½ cups cider vinegar
1½ cups sugar
1 tablespoon dry mustard
1 teaspoon ground turmeric
½ teaspoon ground ginger
1 teaspoon mustard seeds
1 teaspoon celery seeds

1. Combine the vegetables in a large colander

BLACK WALNUTS

Walnut Hill didn't get its name for no reason: There are three ancient and towering black walnut trees going down the hill alongside the house. Just so no one forgets they're there, these native American trees begin dropping their hard green nuts sometime in August. (While working in the garden, I've been bopped on the bean more than once!) And the sound of heavy nuts hitting the roof is not subtle. I'm used to it by now, but one night late last summer I was awakened by a somewhat hysterical houseguest banging on my door to alert me that "someone's climbing around on the roof!"

In addition to causing a ruckus, black walnuts aren't the easiest things in the world to open (the squirrels have an easier time getting into them than I do) and they can leave a dark stain everywhere. But all the aggravation is worth it just to be able to have such easy access to the nuts for the earthy flavor they add to cakes (page 180) and pies (page 140). Widely available cultivated English walnuts can be substituted in the recipes, but they're pretty bland compared to their wild cousins. If you can't find a source for black walnuts, you're welcome to come

on over to my house—I've got plenty to spare!

If you can't find them at the market but you come across a black walnut tree, here's how to husk black walnuts (just keep reminding yourself that the results of your labors will be worth it): Set up a work area outdoors on the lawn by placing a board across sawhorses. Put on rubber gloves and wear old clothes. One nut at a time, bang with a hammer until the green outer hull breaks open, then pull it away. Spread the husked nuts out on the lawn, then hose them down to rinse them clean. Place the nuts in a single layer in a shallow box or basket and allow to cure in a cool place for 2 to 3 weeks. Now, at last . . . the nuts can be shelled with a nutcracker and picks as you would shell English walnuts.

Here's one bit of black walnut lore I just learned from an Ohio friend: Native Americans, who put none of nature's bounty to waste, made use of not only the nut meats, but the dark hulls as well. Women would soak them in hot water, then use the liquid to rinse their hair, enriching the color and, not incidentally, covering up any strands of gray.

set over a large saucepan, sprinkle with the salt, toss well, and let stand and drain for 4 hours.

2. Rinse out the pan, then combine the vinegar, sugar, mustard, and spices in it. Place over medium-high heat and bring to a boil. Reduce the heat and let the mixture simmer for 10 minutes. Add the vegetables, bring to a simmer again, and cook 10 minutes longer. Turn up the heat and bring the mixture to a rolling boil.

3. Immediately pack the chow chow into 4 sterilized 1-pint jars, leaving ¼-inch headspace, and seal the jars. Process the jars in a boiling-water bath (page 96) for 15 minutes . Allow the jars to cool, dry and label them, and store in a cool dark place. Refrigerate the chow chow after opening.

Cranberry Dessert Wine

MAKES ABOUT 2 QUARTS

Similar to Swedish glogg, this wine cordial is perfect for sipping by the fire on a cold night. An added bonus is the "drunken" berries that are left from making the wine, which are delicious for topping desserts (see step 2).

2 12-ounce bags cranberries
1½ cups sugar
7 cups dry red wine
1 teaspoon whole cloves
2 3-inch strips orange peel
1 cup applejack or Calvados

1. In a large, nonreactive saucepan, combine the berries and sugar. Place over medium heat and cook, stirring constantly, until all the berries pop, 7 to 10 minutes. Add the wine, cloves, and orange peel and raise the heat to medium-high. Bring the mixture to a boil, then remove from the heat. Cover and let stand overnight.

2. Stir in the applejack, then strain the mixture through a sieve lined with a triple thickness of cheesecloth (transfer the berries to jars and save them for serving over pound cake and

Cranberry Dessert Wine is a wonderful treat to have stashed away for the holidays.

ice cream). Pour the mixture into two 1-quart bottles and seal. Let stand for 2 weeks before using.

Raspberry Dessert Wine Substitute 1½ pints raspberries or 2 12-ounce bags unsweetened frozen raspberries, thawed, for the cranberries and substitute lemon rind for the orange rind; omit the cloves; cook 10 minutes.

Blueberry Dessert Wine Substitute 1½ pints blueberries for the cranberries and substitute lemon rind for the orange rind; replace the cloves with a broken cinnamon stick; cook 10 minutes.

A Harvest Time Get-Together

FOR 20

ℰ

MENU

Shredded Beef Barbecue
Sandwiches

Horseradish-Mustard Sauce

Corn Roasted in the Husk

"Mexican" Cole Slaw

Baked Beans with
Smoked Sausage

Aunt Edna's Potato Salad
with Boiled Dressing

Carrot Salad with
Lemon-Tarragon Dressing

• • •

Chocolate Beet Cake

Pear Ginger Cake

Squash-Raisin Spice Cookies

A crisp fall afternoon spent at a local farm pumpkin picking and taking a hayride (left and opposite) helps to work up a hearty appetite.

Years ago, all the farmers in one area would get together at harvest time to help one another gather their produce, and after the work was done the farm families would gather for a big ox roast and potluck. There would be hayrides for the kids, games (such as horseshoe pitching), and races (potato sack, egg-in-a-spoon, three-legged, and so on). And after dark, a big sing-along around a big bonfire. Now the ox roasts have evolved into community harvest celebrations, sponsored by local fire departments and churches and accompanied by parades and other special events.

Here's an at-home version of one of those get-togethers, featuring beef barbecue (cooked in the oven) and old and new versions of a few pot-luck favorites. You have to supply your own fun and games.

Getting Ready The cookies and the sauce for the sandwiches can be made several days in advance and the cake can be made a day in advance. The barbecue tastes best made a day ahead; see the recipe for reheating. The slaw and other salads can also be made the day before.

The pear cake is best made no sooner than early in the day. The beans can be begun early in the day and allowed to bake most of the day (or bake them the day before, cool, and refrigerate; reheat them in a moderate oven). The corn should be roasted just before serving.

Serve with cider (hard cider, too) and beer, with pots of hot coffee to go with dessert.

THE OX ROAST — THE MIDWESTERN "CLAMBAKE"

If you've ever been to a real seaside clambake, where the food is cooked in a pit lined with hot coals and rocks, you can get the general idea of the ox roasts we have back home.

The method of doing the ox roast itself has changed very little over the years. The night before, the men dig a long, deep pit in a field and a log fire is begun. Once the coals are hot and smoldering, they're covered with a layer of sand. Huge slabs of beef (years ago it was really ox meat), carefully wrapped in foil to retain the juices, are laid on the sand. Heavy steel pipes are laid across the trench then covered with sheets of steel and an insulating layer of earth. In the morning the meat packets are dug up and taken inside where the meat is shredded and mixed with the juices by the women, then kept warm in big kettles, ready for making sandwiches.

Once the fire is going (top), the meat goes in and the pit is covered (above).

Shredded Beef Barbecue

✌

MAKES ENOUGH FOR 20 TO 30 SANDWICHES

This is my home-cooked version of the way ox roasts are done back home. Serve this on store-bought soft onion rolls with shredded iceberg lettuce, if you'd like, and Horseradish-Mustard Sauce.

- 10 pounds lean boneless beef (a combination of round and chuck), cut into 2-inch chunks
- 4 tablespoons olive oil
- 2 medium onions, finely chopped
- 4 large garlic cloves, finely chopped
- ½ cup cider vinegar
- 1 cup well-seasoned beef stock
- 1 12-ounce can dark beer
- 2 tablespoons prepared horseradish
- 1 teaspoon salt
- 1 teaspoon coarsely ground black pepper
- 1 teaspoon red pepper flakes
- 3 dozen soft onion rolls
- Horseradish-Mustard Sauce (recipe follows)

1. Preheat the oven to 325°F.

2. In a large bowl, combine the beef, oil, onions, and garlic and toss well. In batches, transfer the mixture to a large skillet over medium-high heat, brown the meat on all sides, then transfer to a large roasting pan. Pour the vinegar, the beef stock, and the beer into the pan, then add the horseradish, salt, and peppers. Toss well.

3. Cover the pan and roast, tossing every half hour or so, until the meat is very tender and falling apart, about 3 hours. Remove the cover during the last hour of roasting. Take the pan from the oven and allow the meat to cool enough to be easily handled.

4. Remove the meat from the pan to a cutting board. Using two large forks, pull the meat into coarse shreds. Return the meat to the pan and stir it and the pan juices together. Allow to cool, cover the pan, and refrigerate overnight. *(Can be made up to two days in advance and refrigerated, or well in advance and frozen.)*

5. Bring the meat to room temperature, then reheat in a 350°F. oven for 1 hour, stirring once or twice.

Horseradish- Mustard Sauce

&

MAKES 4 CUPS

2 cups good-quality mayonnaise
½ pint sour cream
½ cup prepared English mustard
½ cup prepared horseradish
½ teaspoon salt

Combine all the ingredients in a mixing bowl, mix well, and refrigerate for 4 hours or overnight to allow the flavors to blend. *(The sauce can be made several days in advance.)*

Corn Roasted in the Husk

&

1. Remove the dark outer leaves from the husks and soak the corn (1 to 2 ears per person) in water for 2 hours. Carefully pull back the inner leaves, remove the silk, and spread the corn lightly with softened butter. Pull the leaves back over the corn and tie them closed at the end, using thin strips cut from the outer leaves as ties.

2. Oven method Preheat the oven to 400°F. Arrange the corn in a single layer in a shallow baking pan. Roast 20 to 30 minutes.

Grill method Prepare the ears of corn as above and arrange the corn in a single layer on a grill about 2 inches above hot, ash-covered coals. Cover loosely with foil and grill, turning once or twice, for 15 to 20 minutes.

A home-cooked version of the ox-roast and roasted corn (above) and an array of salads and baked beans (right).

"Mexican" Cole Slaw

৯৯

SERVES 16 TO 20

Here's an unusual slaw, flavored with tomatoes, onions, and peppers. Try heaping some onto the barbecue sandwiches. If really good red-ripe tomatoes are unavailable, use the best you can find and add a tablespoon of tomato paste to the dressing. If you like it hot, you might also want to add a bit more hot sauce, too.

Dressing

3 medium, very ripe tomatoes, seeded and
    coarsely chopped
3 roasted red bell peppers, coarsely
    chopped
¼ cup red wine vinegar
⅔ cup olive oil
½ teaspoon salt
¼ cup sugar
1 teaspoon hot pepper sauce
2 large garlic cloves

• • •

1 large head (about 3 pounds) green
    cabbage, thinly shredded
1 green bell pepper, chopped
1 medium onion, very thinly sliced
3 stalks celery, thinly sliced
    diagonally

1. In the bowl of a food processor fitted with the steel chopping blade, combine all the dressing ingredients. Process until the tomatoes and peppers are coarsely pureed.

2. Combine the cabbage, pepper, onion, and celery in a large bowl. Pour the dressing over the vegetables and toss. Cover and refrigerate for 4 hours before serving.

Baked Beans with Smoked Sausage

৯৯

SERVES 16 TO 20

A variation on traditional, long-baked beans, with a little garlic, apple, ginger, and rum.

1 1-pound bag dried red kidney beans,
    picked over and rinsed
1 1-pound bag dried pea beans, picked
    over and rinsed
1 tablespoon salt
1 pound kielbasa, diagonally cut into
    ½-inch slices
3 medium onions, chopped
2 10-ounce packages frozen lima beans,
    thawed
2 medium baking apples, peeled, cored,
    and chopped
2 tablespoons grated gingerroot
4 large garlic cloves, chopped
¾ cup molasses
¾ cup tomato puree
½ cup prepared Dijon mustard
½ cup dark rum

1. Place the kidney beans, pea beans, and salt in a large saucepan and add water to cover by 2 inches. Place over high heat and bring to a rolling boil. Boil for 2 minutes, turn off the heat, cover the pan, and let stand 1 hour.

2. Place the sausage in a large, heavy skillet with 2 tablespoons water. Place over medium heat and cook, stirring occasionally to prevent sticking, until the sausage begins to render its fat, about 10 minutes. Add the onions and continue cooking until the onions are golden and the sausage is well browned, about 10 minutes longer. Remove from the heat and reserve.

3. Preheat the oven to 350°F. Drain the soaked beans, reserving the cooking liquid. Place the beans in a deep 6-quart baking dish or beanpot and add the lima beans, apples, ginger, and garlic. Transfer the sausage mixture to the baking dish and stir to mix all the ingredients together.

4. In a spouted bowl or large measuring cup, combine the molasses, tomato puree, mustard, and rum and stir to blend. Pour this mixture evenly over the bean mixture. Add enough reserved bean cooking liquid to just cover the beans. Cover the dish tightly with aluminum foil.

5. Place the dish in the oven and bake for 1½ hours, then turn the heat down to 275°F. and

continue baking for 6 hours more. Add more bean liquid or water, periodically to keep the beans moist during baking. Serve hot or warm. *(This can be made a day in advance and refrigerated; reheat in a 300° F. oven for 1½ hours.)*

Aunt Edna's Potato Salad with Boiled Dressing

℘

SERVES 16

Before jarred mayonnaise became widely available, "boiled" dressings were the basis for potato and macaroni salads and coleslaw. Aunt Edna's potato salad, one that has gotten rave reviews for years, is a typical one back home, with boiled dressing, lots of hard-boiled egg, and a touch of sweet pickle relish.

Dressing

2 large eggs
1 teaspoon dry mustard
1 tablespoon sugar
½ teaspoon salt
⅛ teaspoon cayenne pepper
¼ teaspoon mild paprika
2 tablespoons all-purpose flour
¼ cup water
¼ cup cider vinegar
2 tablespoons butter, softened
¼ cup milk

• • •

8 cups thickly sliced cooked potatoes
2 medium onions, chopped
3 stalks celery, diced
1 tablespoon sweet pickle relish
3 hard-boiled eggs, coarsely chopped
1 hard-boiled egg, sliced
1 medium tomato, cut into wedges
Paprika

1. In the top of a double boiler (not yet over simmering water), whisk the eggs until frothy and lemon-colored. In a small mixing bowl, stir together the mustard, sugar, salt, cayenne, paprika, and flour, then whisk this mixture into the eggs. Whisk in the water and vinegar.

2. Place the pan over simmering water and cook, whisking constantly, until the mixture becomes thick and lumpy, about 7 minutes. Continue whisking until the mixture becomes smooth, 3 or 4 minutes longer, then whisk in the butter. Remove from the heat and allow to cool.

3. Whisk in the milk, then transfer the dressing to a small bowl or jar, cover, and chill 2 hours.

4. In a large bowl, combine the potatoes, onions, celery, relish, and chopped eggs in a mixing bowl. Pour the dressing over all and toss to coat. Chill several hours. Garnish with the sliced egg and tomato and sprinkle with paprika.

Carrot Salad with Lemon-Tarragon Dressing

℘

SERVES 16 TO 20

Dressing

½ cup olive oil
¼ cup vegetable oil
1/4 cup white wine vinegar
Juice of 2 lemons
1 garlic clove, chopped
1 tablespoon chopped tarragon *or*
    ½ teaspoon dried tarragon
¼ cup chopped parsley
2 teaspoons sugar
½ teaspoon salt
½ teaspoon finely ground black pepper

• • •

5 pounds carrots, thinly sliced diagonally
1 medium red onion, thinly sliced

1. Combine the dressing ingredients in a jar, cover tightly, and shake well.

2. Place the carrots in a large saucepan and add salted water to cover. Place over medium heat and bring to a boil. Cook the carrots until crisp-tender, 10 to 15 minutes, and drain.

3. Transfer the carrots to a mixing bowl, add the onion, and pour the dressing over them. Cover and refrigerate several hours or overnight.

Chocolate Beet Cake

ℰℬ

MAKES ONE 10-INCH TUBE CAKE

An exceptionally rich and moist chocolate cake, with a nice redding-brown color. Don't let on about the secret ingredient.

3 large eggs
1¾ cups sugar
3 ounces (3 squares) semisweet chocolate, melted and cooled
1½ cups mashed cooked beets (see Note)
¼ cup vegetable oil
1 teaspoon vanilla extract
2 cups all-purpose flour
2 teaspoons baking powder
1 teaspoon ground cinnamon
¼ teaspoon salt
Confectioners' sugar, for dusting

1. Preheat the oven to 375°F. Grease a 10-inch tube pan or Bundt pan and dust it with flour.

AUTUMN CHORES

- Repairing and repainting fences
- Pickling and preserving
- Drying herbs and flowers
- Planting bulbs
- Sealing the driveway
- Cleaning out the planting pots on the terrace and putting them away
- Cleaning and taking down the window boxes
- Protecting tender plants for the winter
- Reseeding any bare patches in the grass
- Washing the storm windows
- Cleaning and storing outdoor furniture
- Inspecting the weather stripping around windows and doors and repairing if necessary
- Gathering black walnuts from the lawn
- Storing firewood
- Raking leaves, raking leaves, raking leaves!

2. In a mixing bowl, beat the eggs and sugar together until thick and lemon-colored. Add the chocolate, beets, and oil and beat until well blended, then beat in the vanilla. In a separate bowl, sift together the flour, baking powder, cinnamon, and salt. Beat the dry ingredients into the wet mixture and continue beating until very well blended, about 2 minutes.

3. Transfer the batter to the prepared pan and bake until a toothpick or cake tester inserted in the center of the cake comes out clean, 45 to 50 minutes. Place the pan on a wire rack and cool the cake in the pan for 20 minutes. Then remove the cake from the pan to the rack and allow to cool completely. Dust the cake lightly with confectioners' sugar before serving.

Note: One 16-ounce can sliced beets, drained, will yield approximately this amount.

Pear Ginger Cake

ℰℬ

MAKES ONE 9 X 13-INCH CAKE

Chopped preserved ginger in the batter gives this cake a wonderfully intense flavor. The ginger, jarred in syrup, is available in the Oriental section of large supermarkets or in Oriental food shops.

2 cups flour
4 teaspoons baking powder
½ teaspoon salt
¼ cup sugar
½ cup vegetable shortening
1 large egg, lightly beaten
1 cup milk
2 tablespoons finely chopped preserved ginger

Topping
5 to 6 cups peeled and sliced Bosc or Anjou pears
1 cup sugar
1 teaspoon ground cinnamon
½ teaspoon ground ginger
2 teaspoons cornstarch
½ cup (1 stick) butter, melted

These homey old-time desserts have a few surprises in store.

1. In a large mixing bowl, sift together the flour, baking powder, salt, and sugar, then cut in the shortening. Add the egg and milk and stir until the dry ingredients are just moistened, then stir in the ginger.

2. Preheat the oven to 375°F. Spread the batter evenly into a 9 x 13-inch pan (or a shallow oval baking dish of similar proportions). Arrange the pear slices on the batter, overlapping them slightly. Combine the sugar, cinnamon, ginger, and cornstarch and sprinkle this mixture over the pears. Drizzle the melted butter over all.

3. Bake until the pears are nicely browned and glazed and a cake tester inserted in the center of the cake comes out clean, 45 minutes. Remove the pan to a wire rack and cool the cake in the pan. Serve cut into squares.

Squash – Raisin Spice Cookies

ৡ৯

MAKES ABOUT 6 DOZEN

¾ cup vegetable shortening
1 cup firmly packed light brown sugar
2 large eggs
1 teaspoon vanilla extract

2¼ cups all-purpose flour
½ teaspoon baking soda
1 teaspoon baking powder
½ teaspoon salt
2½ teaspoons ground cinnamon
1 teaspoon ground ginger
½ teaspoon ground cloves
½ teaspoon grated nutmeg
1¼ cups grated yellow summer squash
   or zucchini
1½ cups raisins
1½ cups chopped walnuts
Confectioners' sugar, for dusting

1. Preheat the oven to 375°F. Lightly grease baking sheets or line them with parchment.

2. In a mixing bowl, cream the shortening and brown sugar together until light and fluffy, then beat in the egg and vanilla. In a separate bowl, sift together the flour, baking soda, baking powder, salt, and spices. Beat the dry mixture into the wet mixture, then stir in the zucchini, raisins, and nuts.

3. Drop the dough by teaspoonfuls about 2 inches apart onto the prepared baking sheets. Bake until the edges are lightly browned, 8 to 10 minutes. Remove the cookies to wire racks to cool, then dust generously with confectioners' sugar. Store the cookies in tightly covered containers.

An Old-Ohio Country Dinner

FOR 8

ℛ

MENU

Tomato and Sage Fritters

• • •

Stuffed Pork Chops with Bread and Potato Dressing

Pink Applesauce (page 101)

Squash and Pear Chutney (page 100)

Roasted Carrots and Parsnips with Pepper and Herbs

Sautéed Spiced Red Cabbage

• • •

Ohio Lemon Pie

Dried Apricot—Molasses Cake

W hen I was growing up and we had pork chops with an herb-flavored stuffing for dinner and sliced lemon pie for dessert, I had no idea that these were traditional Shaker dishes that had spread across our region. The Shakers, who were a fixture in northern Ohio, as well as other areas, throughout the nineteenth century, created the first "new American" cuisine. They used traditional methods for cooking fresh native produce—fruits, vegetables, and herbs—and combined them in simple but original ways. And even when the harvest had passed, there was still always an emphasis on flavor.

Also among the early Ohio settlers were the Amish and Mennonites, who have the most pristine farms anywhere and a simple, wholesome style of living. (Many years ago, when a tornado ripped destruction through our area, an army of our Mennonite neighbors from the next county were the first to arrive on the scene with mountains of food and willing hands to do whatever was needed to help us clean up and start to rebuild.) The Amish and Mennonite influence on

The back porch, with a ceiling full of baskets and walls hung with samplers, is a cozy spot for a casual dinner (opposite).

112

cooking has been much like that of the Shakers, with the same emphasis on simplicity, freshness, and flavor, and this dinner reflects those wholesome qualities.

Getting Ready The Pink Applesauce and Dried Apricot Cake can both be made up to a day in advance (or make the applesauce well in advance and can it as explained in the recipe). Ready the lemon slices for the pie the night before serving.

Early in the day, assemble and bake the pie, make the batter for the tomato fritters, pare the carrots and parsnips, shred the cabbage, and make the stuffing.

About an hour before serving time, begin assembling the chops and have the roasted vegetable dish ready to go into the oven with the chops.

Start cooking the cabbage about 10 minutes before serving time.

Serve cider, a fruity Zinfandel, or a dry Johannisberg Riesling with the first and main courses, and strong, hot tea with dessert.

Tomato and Sage Fritters

ℱℬ

SERVES 6 TO 8

Here's a recipe for the times long after the fresh tomatoes are gone and you're still craving tomato flavor.

1 ½ cups canned tomato puree
½ cup tomato paste
3 large eggs, well beaten
1 cup very fine cracker crumbs
¼ cup all-purpose flour
1 teaspoon sugar
¼ teaspoon salt
⅛ teaspoon freshly ground black pepper
3 scallions, white and green parts, finely chopped
3 tablespoons chopped sage *or*
    3 tablespoons chopped parsley and
    ½ teaspoon dried sage

Tomato fritters, flavored with the pungence of fresh sage, are served on a Fire-King platter.

Vegetable oil, for frying
Sage leaves or sprigs of flat-leaf parsley,
for garnish

1. In a mixing bowl, combine the tomato puree, tomato paste, and eggs and mix well. In a separate bowl, combine the cracker crumbs, flour, sugar, salt, and pepper. Add the dry mixture to the wet mixture and stir until the dry ingredients are just moistened, then stir in the scallions and sage. *(The batter can be prepared early in the day, then refrigerated until needed.)*

2. Pour oil into a skillet to a depth of ⅛ inch. Place over medium-high heat and heat the oil to sizzling. Drop the tomato batter by tablespoonfuls into the oil and fry until golden brown, turning to brown both sides. Remove the fritters to a plate lined with absorbent paper and keep warm while using the rest of the batter.

3. To serve, arrange the warm fritters on a platter and garnish with sage leaves or parsley.

Stuffed Pork Chops with Bread and Potato Dressing

SERVES 6

6 double-thick pork loin chops, slit almost to the bone to make a pocket for stuffing (have the butcher do this)
Bread and Potato Dressing (recipe follows)
2 to 3 tablespoons vegetable oil
½ cup apple juice, approximately

1. Fill the pockets of the chops with the stuffing mixture and secure with toothpicks. (Any leftover stuffing can be placed in a small greased baking dish, covered, and baked along with the chops.) Place the vegetable oil in a large skillet, over medium-high heat until sizzling. A few at a time, lightly brown the pork chops on both sides.

2. Preheat the oven to 375°F. Lightly oil a large shallow roasting pan or baking dish (preferably

CORNHUSK WREATH

Here's how to make the cornhusk wreath hanging next to the back door. Two or three at a time, carefully remove the husks from dried ears of corn. One at a time, fold the husks in half end to end. Wrap 8-inch lengths of thin wire around the ends of the husks and then poke the wires into a storebought straw wreath to cover the front and sides. (A 12-inch wreath will need the husks from about 2 dozen ears of corn). Decorate by wiring on dried yarrow or any other flowers, wheat, reeds, and bitterberries.

one that can be brought to the table) that will hold the chops in one layer.

3. Arrange the chops closely together in the roasting pan and pour the apple juice over them. Cover the baking dish with its lid or aluminum foil and roast the chops 25 minutes. Turn the chops and roast uncovered until the meat is well browned, about 20 minutes longer. Add a bit more apple juice if necessary.

4. Serve the chops from the baking dish, with the pan juices spooned over each portion.

Bread and Potato Dressing

ℰ

SERVES 6

¼ cup (½ stick) butter
2 medium onions, chopped
½ cup diced celery
2 carrots, finely diced
3 medium boiling potatoes, finely diced
1 Golden Delicious or Granny Smith apple, peeled, cored, and diced
2 tablespoons chopped parsley
½ teaspoon rubbed sage
½ teaspoon dried thyme
⅛ teaspoon salt
¼ teaspoon freshly ground black pepper
3 cups soft cubes white bread
1 large egg, lightly beaten
1 cup chicken or pork stock

1. In a large, heavy skillet, melt the butter over medium heat. Add the onions, celery, carrots, and potatoes, and sauté until the onions are golden and translucent and the other vegetables are tender, 10 to 12 minutes. Stir in the apple, herbs, salt, and pepper and sauté 5 minutes longer.

2. In a large mixing bowl, combine the bread crumbs and the skillet mixture and toss to combine. Add the egg and stock and toss again. Cover and refrigerate a few hours to allow the flavors to blend. Do not stuff the dressing into the meat until just before cooking.

Roasted Carrots and Parsnips with Pepper and Herbs

ℰ

SERVES 6

Long cooking with pepper and herbs gives these root vegetables a wonderful, earthy flavor. And once they're in the oven, they can bake right along with the pork chops, requiring almost no attention at all.

¾ pound carrots, peeled and thinly sliced on the diagonal
½ pound parsnips, peeled and thinly sliced on the diagonal
2 tablespoons (¼ stick) butter
⅓ cup hot chicken stock
1 teaspoon chopped basil *or* ½ teaspoon dried basil
2 tablespoons chopped flat-leaf parsley
½ teaspoon salt
¼ teaspoon coarsely ground black pepper
Chopped basil and/or flat-leaf parsley, for garnish

Preheat the oven to 375°F. Arrange the carrots and parsnips in a buttered, shallow, 1½-quart baking dish and dot with butter. In a measuring cup, combine the stock, herbs, salt, and pepper. Pour the stock mixture over all, cover, and bake, turning once or twice, until the vegetables are very tender, 50 to 60 minutes. Serve hot, garnished with chopped herbs.

Dinner is served family style (above).

Fall colors and flavors: Stuffed pork chops with Pink Applesauce, roasted carrots and parsnips, and spicy red cabbage (below).

Sautéed Spiced Red Cabbage

SERVES 6

This steam-sautéed cabbage is a bit of a surprise, crisp-tender and nicely seasoned with mustard and cumin.

- 2 tablespoons butter
- 1 small head red cabbage (about 1 pound), very coarsely chopped
- 1 medium onion, chopped
- ¼ teaspoon ground cumin
- ¼ teaspoon dry mustard
- 2 tablespoons cider vinegar
- 2 tablespoons light brown sugar
- Salt and freshly ground black pepper

Melt the butter in a heavy saucepan over medium heat. Add the cabbage, onion, cumin, and mustard. Sprinkle the vinegar over the vegetables and toss well. Cover the pan and cook, stirring occasionally, until the cabbage is crisp-tender, 5 to 7 minutes. Stir in the sugar, season to taste with salt and pepper, cook 1 minute longer, and serve.

Ohio Lemon Pie

❦

MAKES ONE 9-INCH PIE

A lemon lover's dream, with pure, unadulterated lemon flavor, this old Shaker recipe is an unusual alternative to the more usual lemon meringue pie.

    3 lemons
    3 cups sugar
    Double recipe Basic Pastry (page 85)
    6 large eggs, well beaten
    Milk and sugar

1. Grate the yellow rind from the lemons into a mixing bowl, then peel off and discard the white pith. Slice the lemons very thinly and add the slices and sugar to the bowl. Toss well, cover, and refrigerate 8 hours or overnight.

2. Preheat the oven to 425°F. Line a 9-inch pie pan with half the pastry. Layer the lemon slices into the pie pan and pour the 6 beaten eggs evenly over them. Top with the remaining pastry and seal and crimp the edges. Cut long slashes in the pastry to allow steam to escape while baking. Brush the pastry with milk and sprinkle generously with sugar.

3. Bake for 10 minutes, reduce the heat to 325°F., and bake until a knife inserted into the pie comes out clean and the crust is golden brown, 35 to 40 minutes. Remove to a wire rack to cool.

One of the neighbors helps himself to dinner in one of the walnut trees (above).

A choice of two desserts (opposite) is a nice indulgence every now and then.

Dried Apricot – Molasses Cake

❦

MAKES ONE 10-INCH
TUBE CAKE

D ried apricots give this moist, spicy, gingerbreadlike cake an unexpected flavor. The dried apricots available in health food stores or in the bulk food sections of some grocery stores are preferable to the prepackaged kind.

    1 cup chopped dried apricots
    ⅔ cup molasses
    Grated rind of 1 small orange
    ¾ cup buttermilk
    1 cup sugar
    1 large egg
    2½ cups all-purpose flour
    ½ teaspoon salt
    2 teaspoons baking soda
    1½ teaspoons ground cinnamon
    1½ teaspoons ground ginger
    ½ teaspoon ground cloves
    ½ teaspoon grated nutmeg
    Confectioners' sugar, for dusting

1. Combine the apricots and the molasses in a small, heavy saucepan. Place over medium heat and bring to a simmer. Reduce the heat and simmer the mixture gently for 5 minutes. Stir in the orange rind, remove from the heat, and cool.

2. Preheat the oven to 350°F. Grease a 10-inch tube pan.

3. In a mixing bowl, combine the buttermilk, sugar, and egg and beat until smooth. In a separate bowl, combine the flour, salt, baking soda, and spices and blend well. Gradually beat the dry mixture into the wet mixture. Add the molasses mixture and beat until well blended.

4. Transfer the batter to the prepared pan and bake until the edges of the cake come away from the pan and a toothpick or cake tester comes out clean, about 30 minutes. Cool 10 minutes in the pan, then remove from the pan and cool on a wire rack. Dust with confectioners' sugar before serving.

An Indian Summer Supper

FOR 6

℘

MENU

Autumn Hazes
(with or without rum)

Popcorn

• • •

Corn, Potato, and Cabbage
Chowder

Pepper-Glazed Baked
Ham Sandwiches on Caraway
Black Bread (page 38)
with "Hot-as-Hades"
Pepper Jam (page 100) or
Hot Garlicky Honey Mustard

• • •

Devil's Food Jumbles

Apples Out-of-Hand

In early October, there are always those precious few days of Indian summer, when warm daytime weather returns. Everyone's out and doing all the things that need to be done all at once in the fall: raking leaves and more leaves, putting summer furniture away, and cleaning up the garden. With everyone so busy, it seems like a good time to issue impromptu invitations, asking the guests to drop by at seven for supper.

The point here is to have a meal that can be prepared in an hour or two. Though the days are warm, the evenings cool off quickly, so after a relaxing drink, a hearty soup and sandwiches are a good bet, with just-baked cookies and seasonal apples for dessert.

Getting Ready The meal can be put together in 1½ to 2 hours if you use store-bought bread for the sandwiches, which is perfectly okay for an impromptu supper. If you've planned in advance, the bread can be baked well ahead of time and frozen.

First bake the cookies (a few days ahead or anytime during the day). Next get the ham into the oven (if you don't have any homemade pepper jam on hand, store-bought will do in a pinch. Use a good store-bought honey mustard, too, or make the recipe below a day or so before.

The soup will take about 45 minutes, but it doesn't require constant attention; it can also be made anytime during the day and reheated just before serving.

Mix the drinks at serving time.

On a cool night, a simple supper is served in the living room (opposite). A fire is glowing and the mantel is decorated for fall.

Autumn Hazes (with or without rum)

ℰ

For each drink, fill a tall glass halfway with ice. Add ½ ounce dark rum if using, then fill the glass ¾ full with cider. Add a generous splash of ginger ale and stir with a cinnamon stick.

Corn, Potato, and Cabbage Chowder

ℰ

SERVES 6

¼ cup (½ stick) butter
3 medium onions, coarsely chopped
2 carrots finely diced
2 stalks celery, diced
4 cups peeled diced potatoes
4 cups chicken stock
4 cups coarsely shredded cabbage
2 cups lowfat milk
2 10-ounce packages frozen corn kernels, thawed
2 tablespoons chopped parsley
2 teaspoons thyme leaves *or* ½ teaspoon dried thyme
Salt and coarsely ground black pepper

1. Melt the butter in a Dutch oven over medium heat, then add the onions, carrot, and celery. Sauté until the onions are golden, 7 to 10 minutes. Add the potatoes and chicken stock to the pan and bring to a boil. Reduce the heat to low and simmer 10 minutes.

2. With a slotted spoon, remove 2 cups of the vegetables from the pot and transfer to the bowl of a food processor fitted with the steel chopping blade. Add 1 cup of the cooking liquid to the processor bowl and puree the mixture until smooth. Return the pureed mixture to the pot and stir until blended in.

3. Add the cabbage, raise the heat to medium, and bring the mixture to a boil. Reduce the heat to low and simmer 5 minutes. Add the milk, corn, parsley, and thyme, bring to a simmer

again, and cook 10 minutes, stirring occasionally to prevent sticking. Season to taste with salt and pepper and serve hot. (*The soup can be made a day in advance and refrigerated; reheat slowly over low heat.*)

Pepper-Glazed Baked Ham

ℰ

A precooked ham is one of the easiest things in the world to deal with. The trimming takes a few minutes time, but once the ham is in the oven there's almost nothing to do. Use either a bone-in butt-end ham or a boneless ham.

1. Preheat the oven to 325°F.

2. Cut the hard rind from a precooked ham. Trim the fat to a thickness of 1/8 inch and score the fat. Place the ham on a rack in a shallow roasting pan and bake for 1 hour.

3. In a small, heavy saucepan, melt a cup or so of "Hot-as-Hades" Pepper Jam (page 100) over low heat. Brush the jam generously over the ham and continue baking the ham until it is heated through, total cooking time about 15 to 18 minutes per pound. Allow the ham to cool to room temperature before slicing.

Hot Garlicky Honey Mustard

ℰ

MAKES ABOUT 1½ CUPS

This fiery and sweet mustard is easy to make, so I always a keep a jar in the refrigerator for spreading onto sandwiches, steamed vegetables, and simple grilled meats from chicken to kielbasa.

¾ cup red wine vinegar
¾ cup dry mustard
1 small garlic clove, crushed
⅔ cup honey
2 large egg yolks, at room temperature

INDIAN SUMMER AND SQUAW WINTER

Of the people who worked for Dad on the farm, the one who was the most fascinating to me was Pop Walters. I never knew his first name; everybody always called him Pop. He was an engaging older gentleman with a grainy voice and a quick laugh, and he was a lively storyteller, an expert on folklore.

Pop taught us that in the fall, there must always be Squaw Winter, a cold spell with maybe even the first frost, before the warm weather could return for a brief time to bring Indian Summer. And for it to be truly Indian Summer the leaves have to turn from their summer greens to burnt oranges, deep reds, gold, and brown. Now I don't remember if Pop ever told us how these "seasons" got their names, but I still look forward to them every year.

1. Place the vinegar in a small saucepan and bring to a boil. Remove the pan from the heat and stir in the mustard and garlic. Cover and let stand overnight at room temperature.

2. Remove the garlic clove, then beat in the honey and egg yolks. Place the pan over low heat and cook, stirring constantly, until thickened. Transfer the mustard into 2 half-pint jars or small crocks, cover tightly, and store in the refrigerator. (The mustard will keep up to a month.)

Devil's Food Jumbles

ঞ্চ

MAKES ABOUT 4 DOZEN

⅔ cup (1⅓ sticks) butter, softened, or
⅔ cups vegetable shortening
1⅓ cups firmly packed dark brown sugar
1 large egg
1½ teaspoons vanilla extract
1½ ounces (1½ squares) semisweet
chocolate, melted and cooled

½ cup sour cream
1¾ cups all-purpose flour
1 teaspoon baking powder
½ teaspoon baking soda
½ teaspoon salt
½ teaspoon ground cinnamon
1½ cups coarsely chopped pecans
1½ cups raisins
1½ cups semisweet chocolate chips
Granulated sugar, for sprinkling

1. Preheat the oven to 375°F. Lightly grease baking sheets or line them with parchment.

2. Cream the butter and brown sugar together until light and fluffy, then beat in the egg and vanilla. Next beat in the melted chocolate, then the sour cream. In a separate bowl, sift together the flour, baking powder, baking soda, salt, and cinnamon. Gradually beat the dry ingredients into the wet mixture, then stir in the pecans, raisins, and chocolate chips.

An apple and cookies — sometimes the simplest desserts are the best.

3. Drop by heaping teaspoonfuls about 2 inches apart onto the baking sheets and sprinkle generously with sugar. Bake until the edges are browned, 8 to 10 minutes. Allow to cool 5 minutes on the baking sheets, then transfer to wire racks to cool completely. Pack in tightly covered containers and store in a cool place.

A Lazy Morning Stick-to-the-Ribs Breakfast

FOR 6

ℱ∂

MENU

Cold-Weather Poached Fruit

Steamed Dublin Coddle

Soft-Scrambled Eggs with Chives

Oatmeal Soda Bread

Honey Butter (page 17)

Lemon and Lime Marmalade

Orange Juice   Hot Coffee

There are those Saturday mornings in November when I can hear the wind blowing and pushing low-hanging branches against the side of the house. I know it's cold. I'd rather stay in bed, under the covers, warm and snug. But there are weekend guests to feed, so it's up I get and downstairs I go.

No one's up yet and the house is quiet, so I close the kitchen doors, and start the coffee brewing, and get breakfast on. I still have a few moments to myself, so I sit at the windows in the breakfast room overlooking the yard, watching the squirrels harvesting black walnuts, eating as many as they carry away. The birds are at the feeder having their breakfast, and the hills beyond the yard are golden yellow and scarlet red as the trees take on their autumn colors and . . . time to get back to making breakfast.

When everything's ready, I shout up from the bottom of the stairs, "Get up, you old slugs! No one sleeps past ten on a weekend in this house. You've already missed the best part of the day!" (Well, that's what I want to shout, but everyone can really sleep as long as they like, and breakfast—or even lunch, if it comes to that—is ready whenever they are.)

Getting Ready The fruit can be prepared anytime the day before and either served chilled or rewarmed for a few minutes over low heat.

The Dublin coddle needs to go onto the stove about an hour and a half before serving time; it can also be made a day in advance and refrigerated, then steamed for about 30 minutes to rewarm at serving time. The bread needs to be started about 45 minutes before serving. Neither needs much tending once they're on the stove and in the oven, respectively.

On a lazy fall day when the weather's not up to snuff, a hearty breakfast really fits the bill.

The eggs need to be made just before serving, but they only take a few minutes.

The marmalade can be made well in advance; if you don't want to take the time for homemade, try some of the wonderful store-bought preserves and marmalades that are widely available.

Cold-Weather Poached Fruit

❧

SERVES 6

A colorful combination with rich, comforting flavors. Serve the fruit either warmed or chilled. Toss in a handful of cranberries if you'd like. This makes a good dessert, too; stir in a tablespoon of brandy or bourbon during the last 5 minutes of cooking and serve with a few gingersnaps or Spicy Anise Snaps (page 154).

1 cup apple juice
Juice of 1 lemon
¼ cup firmly packed light brown sugar
1 3- to 4-inch cinnamon stick
¾ cup dried prunes
¾ cup dried apricots
3 to 4 Anjou or Bosc pears, peeled, cored, and quartered
½ teaspoon vanilla extract
Strips of lemon rind, for garnish

1. In a medium, heavy saucepan, combine the juices, sugar, and cinnamon stick. Place over medium-high heat and bring to a boil. Reduce the heat to low, add the prunes and apricots, and simmer gently for 5 minutes. Add the pears and simmer until they are just tender, 10 to 15 minutes. Remove from the heat and carefully stir in the vanilla.

2. Transfer the mixture to a serving bowl, cover, and chill overnight. Garnish with strips of lemon rind before serving.

Steamed Dublin Coddle

&

SERVES 6 TO 8

This is a traditional Irish dish that I first made way back when I lived on New York's Fifth Avenue and hosted a brunch before the St. Patrick's Day Parade. In Ireland, this is a Saturday-night dish, but I like it just as well for a hearty late breakfast. One of the best things about this dish is that, once it's on the stove, it doesn't need any fussing with.

> 1 pound bangers or breakfast sausages
> 6 medium boiling potatoes, quartered
> 4 medium onions, peeled and cut into
>   eighths
> 2 tablespoons chopped parsley
> ¾ pound thickly sliced Irish bacon (see
>   Note)
> 1 12-ounce bottle dark beer

1. Prick the sausages well with a fork. Place them in a skillet over medium heat with a few tablespoons water and brown the sausages well on all sides.

2. In a large kettle fitted with a steamer basket, layer the ingredients in the order listed, ending with a single layer of bacon. Pour the beer into the bottom of the kettle and add water to reach a depth of 1 inch. Cover the kettle and place over medium-high heat. When the beer comes to a boil, reduce the heat so that it simmers gently.

3. Cook, adding more water to the kettle if necessary to maintain a depth of 1 inch, until the potatoes and onions are tender and the bacon and sausages are cooked through, about 1½ hours. Arrange the meats and vegetables on a deep platter and serve.

Note: Irish bacon is more readily available than it once was, but if you can't find it substitute Canadian bacon or a good, lean, smoky country bacon, preferably from a small regional producer.

Soft-Scrambled Eggs with Chives

&

SERVES 6

The addition of cream cheese makes these eggs soft and creamy.

Dublin coddle, scrambled eggs, and a wedge of Oatmeal Soda Bread.

¼ cup (½ stick) butter
1 dozen large eggs
⅓ cup milk
¼ teaspoon salt
¼ teaspoon white pepper
1 3-ounce package cream cheese, cut
   into chunks
1 tablespoon snipped chives
¼ teaspoon salt

1. In the top of a double boiler over simmering water, melt the butter. Remove the double boiler from the heat and allow the butter to cool slightly.

2. Whisk the eggs, milk, salt, and pepper into the pan. Bring the water in the bottom of the double boiler to a simmer again and place the top of the double boiler over the simmering water.

3. Cook the eggs, stirring with a large spoon to prevent sticking, until curds start to form. Add the cream cheese, chives, and salt and continue cooking until the cheese is melted and blended in and all the egg mixture has formed large, soft curds. Remove from the heat, transfer to a warm serving bowl, and serve immediately.

Oatmeal Soda Bread

ℰℷ

MAKES ONE 8-INCH ROUND LOAF

1¾ cups sifted all-purpose flour
2 tablespoons sugar
2 teaspoons baking powder
1 teaspoon baking soda
½ teaspoon salt
¾ cup quick-cooking oats
¼ cup vegetable shortening, chilled
¾ cup golden raisins
2 teaspoons caraway seeds
¾ cup buttermilk
1 large egg, lightly beaten
2 to 3 tablespoons milk

1. Preheat the oven to 375°F. Lightly grease an 8-inch round baking pan.

2. In a mixing bowl, sift together the flour, sugar, baking powder, baking soda, and salt, then stir in the oats. Using two knives or a pastry blender, cut in the shortening until the mixture resembles coarse meal. Stir in the raisins and caraway seeds. Add the buttermilk and egg and mix well to form a soft dough.

3. Form the dough into a ball, flatten slightly, and place in the prepared plan. Cut a large X in the surface of the dough and then brush lightly with milk. Bake until the bread is golden brown, 35 to 40 minutes. Serve warm or at room temperature, cut into wedges, with sweet butter.

Lemon and Lime Marmalade

ℰℷ

MAKES ABOUT 2 PINTS

This green- and yellow-flecked marmalade has a lot of tangy wake-up power.

2 or 3 lemons, halved lengthwise, sliced
   paper-thin crosswise and seeded
   (enough to measure 1½ cups)
2 or 3 limes, halved lengthwise, sliced
   paper-thin crosswise and seeded
   (enough to measure 1½ cups)
4 cups water
4½ cups sugar, approximately

1. Combine the lemons, limes, and water in a heavy, nonreactive saucepan and place over medium-high heat. Bring the mixture to a boil and cook, boiling rapidly, until the fruit is tender, 40 to 50 minutes.

2. Measure the fruit mixture and for each cup of fruit add 1 cup sugar. Return the mixture to a boil and continue cooking until the mixture sheets when dropped from the side of a spoon (220°F. on a candy thermometer), about 30 to 35 minutes.

3. Remove the pan from the heat and cool 15 minutes. Transfer the marmalade to two pint jars or four half-pint jars and cover tightly. Allow to cool completely, then store in the refrigerator.

Supper
After the
Big Event

ℰᕧ

MENU

Chicken, Sausage, and
Vegetable Chili

24-Hour Chopped Salad
with Buttermilk Dressing

• • •

Honey-Baked Apples

**Serving a buffet supper right in the kitchen
(above) keeps things simple and easy.**

In the fall, there are all kinds of events that require getting together, either afterwards or during the event itself: Homecoming Day, an antique show, a craft fair, a school concert, and so on. Back home, the big fall event was the Friday night football game. The grandstand was always full, not only because this was "the only game in town," but because our team, the Willard Flashes, was always pretty good. The marching band always performed at halftime and after the game we'd all go to the school cafeteria for chili and endless and detailed discussion of every play.

Here's a chili supper that can be ready soon after you get home, whatever the event. Everything can be made in advance, and once the chili's heated up, soup's on.

Getting Ready Everything can be prepared in advance and readied with very little fuss. The chili and salad should be made a day in advance; warm the chili over low heat and toss the salad just before serving. The apples are best made no sooner than early on the day they're served; warm in the oven before serving.

The obvious choice with the chili is a light lager beer, then strong, hot tea with dessert.

Chicken, Sausage, and Vegetable Chili

⅌

SERVES 10 TO 12

¼ cup olive oil
2 pounds hot Italian sausage, cut into
    1-inch pieces
12 boneless skinless chicken breast
    halves, cut into 1-inch chunks
2 medium onions, chopped
2 carrots, thinly sliced
2 stalks celery, thinly sliced
2 large green bell peppers, chopped
4 large garlic cloves, finely chopped
¼ cup prepared seasoned chili powder
1 tablespoon ground cumin
3 tablespoons oregano leaves *or* 1½
    teaspoons dried oregano
2 tablespoons thyme leaves *or* 1 teaspoon
    dried thyme
½ teaspoon ground cayenne, or more
    to taste
2 28-ounce cans crushed tomatoes in
    puree
2 cups well-seasoned chicken stock
1 10-ounce package frozen corn kernels
2 16-ounce cans red kidney beans, rinsed
    and drained
2 16-ounce can black beans, rinsed and
    drained
1 16-ounce can white kidney beans
    (cannellini), rinsed and drained
1 16-ounce can chickpeas, rinsed and
    drained
Salt

1. In a large Dutch oven, heat the oil to sizzling over medium heat. Add half the sausage. Sauté the sausage until browned on all sides, remove to absorbent paper, and reserve. Repeat with the remaining sausage and the chicken. Add the onions, carrots, celery, green peppers, and garlic to the pan and sauté until the onions are golden, 5 to 7 minutes.

2. Tilt the pan and, using a large spoon, remove all but about 1 tablespoon fat. Add the spices and herbs and sauté 5 minutes. Add the tomatoes and chicken stock and stir well. Add the reserved chicken and sausage to the pan, and bring the mixture to a simmer.

3. Add the corn and the beans, bring to a simmer again, and cook, stirring occasionally, until the mixture is quite thick, about 45 minutes. Season to taste with salt. Remove the pan from the heat and allow the chili to cool. Cover the pan tightly with its lid or with plastic wrap and chill overnight.

4. Just before reheating, skim off any fat that has risen. Bring the chili to room temperature, then place over low heat and slowly bring to a simmer. Simmer 5 minutes and serve hot.

Chili topped with sour cream and sliced scallions, with a zesty salad on the side.

24-Hour Chopped Salad with Buttermilk Dressing

ℒ

SERVES 10 TO 12

Set out a big bowl of this salad and let everyone decide how they want to eat it: alone with dressing, as a bed for the chili, or piled on top.

Dressing

1 cup buttermilk
1 cup mayonnaise
1 tablespoon lemon juice
2 large garlic cloves, finely chopped
¼ cup snipped chives
¼ cup chopped parsley

1 teaspoon sugar
½ teaspoon salt
¼ teaspoon finely ground black pepper

•••

1 large head iceberg lettuce, coarsely shredded
1 medium red or yellow bell pepper, cut into strips
1 small red onion, thinly sliced and separated into rings
1 head romaine lettuce, coarsely shredded
½ pound Swiss cheese, shredded
1 bunch scallions, white and green parts, cut into ½-inch lengths
1 cup sliced pitted California black olives
1 pint cherry tomatoes, halved
½ pound bacon, cooked crisp and crumbled

HALLOWEEN MEMORIES

Halloween conjures up memories of a hayride around the pastures under a full moon, or a dance at the Zellners' where I learned to square dance, or another party at Patty Wheeler's where I first played "spin the bottle." And there was the Halloween night when I, feeling quite grown-up at ten, took my three-year-old sister trick-or-treating in town. It was pitch-black that night and Betty was scared the whole way; every time someone would answer the door, she would burst into tears. I had no idea how to calm Betty down and by the time we got home, I think I was more frightened than she was.

And then, of course, there are those memories that we all seem to share:

- A row of jack-o'-lanterns
- Bobbing for apples
- Margaret O'Brien in *Meet Me in St. Louis*
- A scarecrow still guarding the spent garden
- Bobbing for apples
- Ghost stories around a bonfire
- Halloween parades
- Cider and doughnuts

Jack-o'-lanterns on a stone wall out back.

In front, wicked witches fly in the trees.

Honey-Baked Apples, just out of the oven, cool down a bit on the kitchen windowsill.

1. In a mixing bowl, combine all the dressing ingredients and whisk to blend. Reserve.

2. The day before serving, layer the salad ingredients into a large serving bowl in the order given, starting with the iceberg lettuce, ending with the cherry tomatoes, and reserving the bacon. Spread the dressing evenly over the top of the salad to cover it completely, then cover the bowl tightly with plastic wrap. Chill overnight.

3. Just before serving, toss the salad to coat it with the dressing, then sprinkle the bacon over the top.

Honey-Baked Apples

୨ə

SERVES 10

I don't like baked apples too fancified, or stuffed with nuts, fruits, and everything else under the sun. A little honey, orange juice, and spice is all they need.

   10 large baking apples, such as Granny
      Smith, Cortland, or Golden Delicious
      (or use a combination)

10 teaspoons butter
10 3- to 4-inch cinnamon sticks
½ cup honey
⅓ cup orange juice
½ teaspoon ground cinnamon
¼ teaspoon grated nutmeg
Sugar
1 cup plain yogurt

1. Preheat the oven to 375°F. Cut the rounded tops from the apples, then core, being careful not to cut all the way through. Arrange the apples in a shallow roasting pan. Place 1 teaspoon butter and 1 cinnamon stick inside each apple.

2. In a measuring cup, combine the honey, orange juice, and spices, then divide the mixture among the apples. Sprinkle the tops of the apples generously with sugar. Pour water into the pan to a depth of ¼ inch. Place the pan in the oven and bake until the apples are tender, about 45 minutes.

3. Remove the pan from the oven and serve warm, in individual dishes, each topped with a dollop of yogurt. *(The apples can be baked early in the day, cooled, covered, and refrigerated; rewarm in a slow oven before serving.)*

My Farmhouse Thanksgiving Dinner

FOR 12 TO 16

❧

MENU

Patchwork Vegetable Pickles
(page 98)

Pickled Baby Beets
(page 98)

Hot Jerusalem
Artichoke Pickle (page 99)

Wild Rice Muffins

• • •

Cider-Glazed Roasted Turkey

Mashed Potatoes with
Giblet and Cider Gravy

Savory Sweet Potato
and Apple Dressing

Cranberry and Onion Relish

Steamed Brussels Sprouts with
Lemon Brown Butter

Huron County Corn Pudding

Joyce's Creamed Green Pumpkin

Oven-Braised Celery
with Shallots

• • •

Black Walnut–Raisin Pie

Maple–Pumpkin Custard Pie

Mom's Pear Dumplings with
Nutmeg Cream

Cranberry Dessert Wine
(page 103)

Back home, our holiday birds always came from Albright's Farm.

The whole family laughs as my turkey passes Mom's watchful eye (opposite).

Thanksgiving on the farm was always a family day, with a big dinner and heartwarming reunions and recollections. The day tended to be long and chatty. The menu featured all the traditional food one thinks of on Thanksgiving, with turkey and dressing, cranberry relish, mashed potatoes, and pies and more pies.

Not long after I moved to New York, my brother, Joe, his wife, Dot, and their kids came for Thanksgiving. We went to Macy's parade, then I gave them a whirlwind tour of the city.

Back at the apartment, I, now a "very sophisticated" New Yorker, served a trendy and complicated menu I thought would wow them. Well, it did. Everything was foreign to them and dinner was a big disappointment for all of us. I had forgotten one of the basic rules of entertaining: Make your guests feel comfortable and at home in your surroundings (and one of the basic rules of life: Don't be a showoff!). Well, I learned my lesson, never to make the same mistake again.

So now in my house, no matter who's coming, I try never to overdo it. There are four unbroken rules when it comes to Thanksgiving: there must be turkey and dressing, cranberries, mashed potatoes, and pumpkin pie. The rest of the menu may vary from year to year, but now it never ventures too far from my Midwestern traditions. And since I rarely get the chance to go back to Ohio for Thanksgiving, I usually find myself hosting an extended family of assorted friends who come from different parts of the country but who all crave an old-fashioned and traditional Thanksgiving dinner.

Getting Ready The cranberry relish can be made well in advance. The day before Thanksgiving, make the dumplings and pies. The celery dish can also be made a day in advance and reheated before serving.

The stuffing should be made early in the day and put into the turkey just before the bird goes into the oven; check the recipe to figure the timing for the turkey, based on its weight. Don't forget to enlist a "volunteer" early on to carve the turkey when it comes out of the oven.

Pare and steam the Brussels sprouts and cook the wild rice for the muffins early in the day. Unless you've got two ovens make the muffins ahead, then rewarm them just before serving.

The corn pudding should be ready to go into the oven about an hour before serving. Next start the potatoes and, when the turkey comes out of the oven, make the gravy. Just before serving time, the celery should be reheated, the muffins warmed, and the Brussels sprouts should be finished.

With dinner, serve a California Gamay Beaujolais or not-too-sweet fresh cider, then the Cranberry Dessert Wine and coffee with dessert.

Wild Rice Muffins

MAKES 1 DOZEN

I like these for breakfast, too, with strawberry preserves. For this menu, it might be a good idea to double the recipe.

⅓ cup wild rice
1⅓ cups water
¼ teaspoon salt
1½ cups all-purpose flour
¼ cup stone-ground yellow cornmeal
2 tablespoons sugar
2 teaspoons baking powder
½ teaspoon salt
¼ teaspoon finely ground black pepper
2 large eggs
¾ cup milk
¼ cup (½ stick) butter, melted and cooled
1 tablespoon finely chopped onion

1. To cook the wild rice, rinse it thoroughly with cold running water, then place in a small, heavy saucepan with the water and salt. Place over medium-high heat and bring to a boil. Reduce the heat to low, cover the pan, and cook until the rice is tender, about 40 minutes. Remove from the heat and cool.

2. Preheat the oven to 400°F. Lightly grease the cups of a 12-cup standard-size muffin pan.

3. In a mixing bowl, sift together the flour, corn-

meal, sugar, baking powder, salt, and pepper. In a separate bowl, beat the eggs lightly with a fork, then add the milk and butter and mix well. Pour the wet mixture over the dry ingredients, then add the wild rice and onion. With the fork, stir all the ingredients together until the dry ingredients are just moistened; do not overmix.

4. Divide the batter among the prepared muffin cups, filling each about ⅔ full. Bake until the muffins are lightly browned, 20 to 25 minutes. Serve hot with sweet butter.

Cider-Glazed Roasted Turkey

℘ℯ

SERVES 16, WITH PLENTY
OF LEFTOVERS

1 20- to 24-pound fresh turkey
Salt and finely ground black pepper
Savory Sweet Potato and Apple Dressing
   (recipe follows)
½ cup (1 stick) butter, melted

Cider Glaze

1½ cups fresh apple cider
1 tablespoon chopped sage *or* 1 teaspoon
   dried rubbed sage
1 tablespoon fresh thyme leaves *or*
   1 teaspoon dried thyme
1 tablespoon grated gingerroot *or* ¾
   teaspoon ground ginger
1 garlic clove, crushed

1. Remove the giblets from the turkey and reserve for gravy. Rinse the turkey well, inside and out, and pat dry with paper towels. Season the cavities and skin with salt and pepper.

2. Preheat the oven to 325°F. Stuff both cavities loosely with stuffing (see Note) and close both ends with trussing skewers and string. Place the turkey, breast side up, on a rack in a large roasting pan. Insert a meat thermometer into the thickest part of the thigh without touching the bone.

3. Soak a 12-inch square double layer of cheese-

cloth in the melted butter and then spread the cheesecloth over the turkey breast. Place the turkey in the oven and roast about 12 minutes per pound, basting every 30 minutes with the pan juices. The turkey will be done when the meat thermometer registers 180°F., or when the juices run clear when the thigh is pricked with a meat fork.

4. Meanwhile, make the glaze by combining all the ingredients in a small saucepan and simmering gently over low heat until the mixture is reduced by half, about 40 minutes. Strain the glaze into a small bowl and reserve.

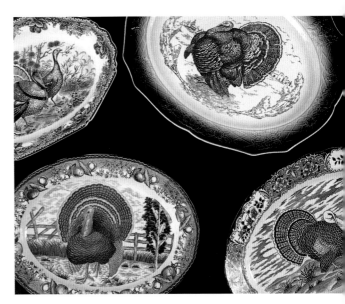

Every year, part of my Thanksgiving morning ritual is trying to decide which turkey platter to use at dinnertime!

5. During the last half hour of roasting, remove the cheesecloth from the turkey and brush the skin liberally with the glaze. Brush every 10 minutes with additional glaze.

6. Remove the finished turkey to a warm platter, cover loosely with aluminum foil, and let it rest for 30 minutes while making the gravy.

Note: Any stuffing that does not fit into the turkey can be packed into a buttered heavy-duty aluminum foil packet and roasted for an hour or so.

Giblet and Cider Gravy

☙

Giblets from the turkey
1 large garlic clove, crushed
¼ teaspoon salt
¼ cup fat skimmed from the roasting pan
¼ cup all-purpose flour
Pan drippings, remaining cider glaze, and enough stock to make 3 cups
Pinch each of dried thyme and rubbed sage
Salt and finely ground black pepper

NEXT-DAY RED FLANNEL TURKEY HASH

I always roast a larger turkey than I need for Thanksgiving dinner, so I'll have plenty of turkey for sandwiches, but when the nice slices are gone, I'm always trying out something new for finishing off the meat (the meaty carcass always gets used for soup). Here's my latest favorite way with leftover turkey.

1 tablespoon butter
1 tablespoon vegetable oil
1½ cups diced unpeeled potatoes
1 small onion, chopped
¼ teaspoon salt
⅛ teaspoon finely ground black pepper
2 cups diced, cooked turkey meat
1 carrot, cooked and diced
1 cup diced, cooked beets (canned beets are fine)
½ cup leftover turkey gravy or light cream

1. Combine the butter and oil in a skillet over medium heat and heat to sizzling. Add the potatoes and onion and sauté until the potatoes are tender and begin to brown, 12 to 15 minutes. Stir in the salt and pepper. Add the turkey, carrot, beets, and gravy and mix well.

2. Pat the mixture down with a spatula. Cover the pan and continue cooking until a brown crust forms on the bottom, 10 to 15 minutes. Cut the hash into wedges and serve.

---

1. While the turkey is roasting, place the giblets, garlic, and salt in a small saucepan with stock or water to cover and place over medium heat. Bring to a simmer, reduce the heat to low, and simmer the giblets until cooked through and very tender, about 45 minutes. Remove the giblets, discard the garlic, reserve the stock, and finely chop the giblets. Cover the giblets and store in the refrigerator until needed.

2. When the turkey is done, skim off the fat from the roasting pan. Place 2 tablespoons of the fat in a medium saucepan over medium heat (discard any remaining fat) and whisk in the flour. Cook, whisking constantly, until the flour is absorbed and a thick paste forms.

3. Scrape the bottom of the roasting pan to remove any browned bits and stir them into the pan juices. Pour the juices into a measuring cup. Add the remaining cider glaze and enough reserved stock to measure 3 cups. Whisk the liquid into the flour-fat mixture until smooth. Add the reserved giblets and the herbs and simmer the gravy until thickened and the flour is cooked, about 7 minutes. Season to taste with salt and plenty of pepper.

Savory Sweet Potato and Apple Dressing

☙

MAKES ABOUT 10 CUPS

Adding sweet potatoes and apples gives Thanksgiving dressing a subtly different but not unfamiliar flavor. It also eliminates the usually gooey and overly sweetened sweet potato casserole from the menu.

½ cup (1 stick) butter
1 bunch scallions, white and green parts, thinly sliced
2 small onions, chopped
1 cup diced celery
3 cups cooked sweet potatoes, diced
3 apples, peeled and diced
4 cups soft white bread cubes
½ cup chopped walnuts, lightly toasted

3 large eggs, lightly beaten
¼ cup chopped parsley
1 teaspoon dried thyme
½ teaspoon rubbed sage
¼ teaspoon grated nutmeg
½ teaspoon salt and ¼ teaspoon freshly
    ground black pepper

1. Melt the butter in a heavy skillet over medium-low heat. Add the scallions, onions, and celery and sauté until the vegetables are crisp-tender, 5 to 7 minutes.

2. Transfer the vegetables to a large mixing bowl. Add the remaining ingredients and toss to combine. Stuff the turkey just before roasting.

Cranberry and Onion Relish

ε&

MAKES ABOUT 4 CUPS

As I was making my grandmother's old-fashioned cranberry relish last November, it occurred to me that it might be interesting to vary it by throwing in an onion and some fresh gingerroot, and here's the result. This makes more than you'll need for Thanksgiving dinner, but it will last in the refrigerator a long time, so you can use it for Christmas dinner, too.

    You can make this relish in a few seconds by pulsing in the food processor but I use an old-fashioned hand-cranked grinder.

1 medium orange
½ lemon
1 medium tart apple
1 medium onion
3 cups (1 12-ounce bag) cranberries
1 1-inch piece gingerroot, peeled and
    coarsely chopped
½ cup sugar
¼ teaspoon ground cloves

1. Quarter the orange and lemon and remove the seeds. Quarter the apple and core it. Do not peel the fruit. Peel and quarter the onion.

2. Grind all the fruit, the onion, and ginger and

I bought these English turkey plates during a visit back home in Ohio.

place them in a bowl. Stir in the sugar and cloves. Cover the bowl and chill for 24 hours before using. *(Can be made well in advance; it keeps indefinitely in the refrigerator.)*

Steamed Brussels Sprouts with Lemon Brown Butter

ε&

SERVES 12

I never liked Brussels sprouts when I was a kid, but I know better now.

3 10-ounce boxes Brussels sprouts,
2 tablespoons butter
Juice of 1 lemon

1. Wash the sprouts well, trim off any tough outer leaves, and halve them. Place them in a steamer over simmering water, and steam until crisp-tender, about 7 to 10 minutes (timing will depend on the age and size of the sprouts). *(Can be steamed in advance and stored in the refrigerator; bring to room temperature before proceeding.)*

2. Melt the butter in a large skillet or wok over medium-low heat. When the butter just begins to brown, add the sprouts and the lemon juice. Cook, tossing constantly, until the sprouts are coated with the butter and lemon juice and heated through, about 3 or 4 minutes. Serve hot.

Huron County Corn Pudding

ℒ

SERVES 10 TO 12

There are lots of corn pudding recipes around, but I like this one best. It's got more corn than most, and it's nicely seasoned with sautéed onions, chives, and herbs.

> 3 tablespoons butter
> 1 medium onion, finely chopped
> 3 tablespoons snipped chives
> 3 cups corn kernels (see Note)
> 3 large eggs, lightly beaten
> 1 teaspoon sugar
> ½ teaspoon salt
> ⅛ teaspoon finely ground black pepper
> 2 cups light cream
> 1 tablespoon all-purpose flour
> A generous pinch each of dried thyme, dried summer savory, and rubbed sage

1. Preheat the oven to 325°F. Generously butter a shallow 2-quart baking dish. In a small skillet over medium-low heat, melt the butter, then add the onion and chives. Sauté until the onion is golden, 5 to 7 minutes. Scrape into a large mixing bowl, getting all the butter.

2. Add the remaining ingredients to the bowl and whisk well to blend. Pour the mixture into the baking dish and carefully place in the oven. Bake until set and lightly browned around the edges, about 50 minutes. Serve warm.

Note: In season, fresh kernels scraped right off the ear is best, but out of season frozen kernels are a good substitute. Place the thawed kernels in the bowl of a food processor and pulse them once or twice to give them that just-scraped texture and to provide a little corn "milk."

Oven-braised celery, gravy in an old turkey-shaped candy dish, wild rice muffins, dressing, pickles, and creamed green pumpkin (top, clockwise from left).

Brussels sprouts with lemon brown butter, cider-glazed turkey, corn pudding, and cranberry and onion relish (left).

Joyce's Creamed Green Pumpkin

ℬ

SERVES 12 TO 16

This unusual recipe, an American adaptation of an old Hungarian dish, comes from my neighbor and friend (and fellow native Ohioan) Joyce Gould. The green in the name doesn't refer to the color—the pumpkins should just be fresh and crisp, and slightly underripe if possible. Joyce always makes a big batch as soon as pumpkins are available at the end of the summer and freezes small batches for later use.

2 small green pumpkins, about 8 inches
    in diameter
Salt
¼ cup (½ stick) butter
1 large onion, chopped
3 tablespoons cider vinegar
2 tablespoons sugar
1 cup tomato sauce
1 tablespoon butter
1 tablespoon flour
1½ cups milk
Salt and finely ground black pepper

1. Peel, seed, and remove the stringy pulp from the pumpkin. Using a coarse grater, grate the pumpkin flesh into long shreds. Place the pumpkin in a large sieve, sprinkle generously with salt, and let stand over a bowl for 30 minutes.

2. Combine ¼ cup butter and onion in a large, heavy pan or Dutch oven over medium heat and sauté until the onion is tender and golden, 7 to 10 minutes. Squeeze the pumpkin shreds firmly to remove all excess water. Add the pumpkin to the pan, along with the vinegar, sugar, and tomato sauce, and mix well. Cover the pan and bring the mixture to a simmer. Reduce the heat to low and simmer until the pumpkin is tender but still crisp, about 20 minutes.

3. Meanwhile, melt 1 tablespoon butter in a small saucepan over low heat, then stir in the flour until absorbed. Add the milk and stir well. Cook, stirring constantly, until the mixture is

slightly thickened and the flour is cooked, about 5 minutes. Add this to the pumpkin mixture and mix well. Season to taste with salt and pepper and serve. *(Can be made a day in advance and refrigerated; reheat in a heavy pan over low heat.)*

Oven-Braised Celery with Shallots

ℬ

SERVES 16

4 small heads celery
1 carrot, finely chopped
6 shallots, finely chopped
¼ cup (½ stick) butter, melted
2 cups hot, well-seasoned chicken stock
2 teaspoons lemon juice
2 teaspoons sugar
Coarsely ground black pepper

1. Preheat the oven to 350°F.

2. Cut the leaves from the celery and reserve. Remove the large outer stalks from the celery and trim the tops so the heads are approximately 6 inches long. (Use the outer stalks and heads in the dressing.) Cut the celery heads in half lengthwise, then cut again to quarter them.

3. Place the celery, cut side down and alternating them head to foot to fit them compactly, into a shallow baking dish just large enough to hold it (approximately 9 x 13 inches). Scatter the chopped carrot and shallots over the celery. In a spouted bowl, combine the butter, stock, lemon juice, and sugar, then pour this mixture over the celery.

4. Cover the baking dish with its lid or with aluminum foil. Place in the oven and bake 1 hour. Remove the cover and bake until the celery is tender and beginning to brown, about 1 hour longer, add black pepper to taste. Serve hot, directly from the baking dish. *(Can be made a day in advance and refrigerated, tightly covered; bring to room temperature and reheat for 30 minutes in a 350°F. oven.)*

Black Walnut – Raisin Pie

❧

MAKES ONE 9-INCH PIE

Black walnuts, native to North America, are especially appropriate on Thanksgiving Day. Their flavor is very intense, so in this pie they're combined with mildly flavored English walnuts and raisins.

Basic Pastry (page 85)
½ cup finely chopped black walnuts
　(see page 102)
½ cup finely chopped English walnuts
1 cup raisins
1 cup firmly packed light brown sugar
¼ cup butter, softened
½ cup dark corn syrup
3 large eggs
1 teaspoon vanilla extract

1. Preheat the oven to 375°F. Line a 9-inch pie pan with the pastry and crimp the edges. In a mixing bowl, toss the 2 kinds of walnuts and the raisins together to mix well, then spread in an even layer over the pastry.

2. In the bowl, cream the brown sugar and butter together until light and fluffy, then beat in the corn syrup, eggs, and vanilla. Pour this mixture into the pan.

3. Bake the pie until the filling is firm, 30 to 40 minutes. Remove to a wire rack to cool.

Maple – Pumpkin Custard Pie

❧

MAKES ONE 9-INCH PIE

A little bit lighter than the more usual pumpkin pie, this still tastes plenty rich.

Basic Pastry (page 85)
¾ cup maple syrup
1½ cups Pumpkin Puree (page 97)
3 large eggs, lightly beaten
1½ cups milk
½ teaspoon salt
1 teaspoon ground cinnamon
1 teaspoon ground ginger
¼ teaspoon ground cloves
¼ teaspoon grated nutmeg

Thanksgiving wouldn't be complete without a few pies and Mom's dumplings.

1. Preheat the oven to 425°F. Line a 9-inch pie pan with the pastry crust.

2. In a mixing bowl, combine all the ingredients and beat until well blended. Pour the mixture into the pie pan.

3. Bake for 8 minutes. Reduce the heat to 350°F. and bake until the top is lightly browned and a knife inserted in the center comes out clean, 35 to 40 minutes. Transfer the pie to a wire rack to cool. Serve chilled or at room temperature.

Mom's Pear Dumplings with Nutmeg Cream

MAKES 12

Mom's dumplings, both apple and pear, have always been among my favorite desserts and I always ask her to make some first thing when she comes for a visit. Most people make dumplings by wrapping the pastry around whole fruit, but I prefer Mom's method of using sliced fruit, which flavors the fruit with more sugar and spice.

> Triple recipe Basic Pastry (page 85)
> 12 medium Anjou or Bosc pears
> ½ cup light brown sugar, approximately
> Ground cinnamon
> Ground ginger
> Grated nutmeg
> Butter
> Milk
> Granulated sugar
> Nutmeg Cream (see below)

1. Divide the pastry dough into two equal portions. On a floured work surface, roll out each portion to a rectangle about 10 x 15 inches and, with a sharp knife, cut each rectangle into six 5-inch squares.

2. Peel, core, and slice the pears and divide the slices into mounds in the center of each pastry square. Sprinkle each pear mound with about 2 teaspoons brown sugar, a generous sprinkling

---

FALL "BOUQUETS"

When the garden stops producing fresh flowers for cutting, there's no need to stop having colorful bouquets around the house. Fall's own "produce" supplies plenty of ingredients. Here are a few ideas:

- A deep oval basket filled with several potted mums

- Dried Indian corn, gourds, and tiny pumpkins in an old wooden dough bowl with grapevines and small branches of fall leaves

- An oddly shaped pumpkin (or a few) for the kitchen table

- A vase filled with dried hydrangeas

- A basket filled with gourds, little pumpkins, and big branches of bittersweet

- A stoneware crock filled with cattails or dried wheat

- Shallow grapevine baskets filled with colorful ornamental kale

---

of cinnamon and ginger, and a pinch of nutmeg. Dot with butter.

3. Preheat the oven to 375°F. Lightly grease baking sheets. Moisten the edges of the pastry with milk. Fold the corners and sides of the pastry up over the center of the pears and pinch all edges together to seal. Don't try to make this too neat—the dumplings should look rather rustic.

4. Place the dumplings on the prepared baking sheets. Brush each dumpling with milk and sprinkle each generously with granulated sugar. Bake until the pastry is nicely browned, about 40 minutes. Remove the pans to wire racks to cool. Remove the dumplings from the pans with a spatula and serve warm with Nutmeg Cream.

Nutmeg Cream

Whip ½ pint heavy cream until soft peaks form, then fold in 2 teaspoons confectioners' sugar, ¼ teaspoon each salt and vanilla, and ⅛ teaspoon grated nutmeg.

An Old and New World Christmas Dinner

FOR 8

ℰ

MENU

Sherried Butternut Squash
and Chestnut Soup

Baking Powder Biscuit Sticks

• • •

Roasted Ducklings
Grandma Stapleton's Way
with Wine Gravy

Spiced Pickled Lady Apples
(page 99)

Cranberry-Herb Dressing

Green Beans with
Caramelized Onions

Bohemian Creamed Cabbage

Baked Turnip and Potato Puree

• • •

Steamed Banana, Date,
and Pineapple Pudding
with Rum Custard Sauce

Hazelnut Fudge Pie

CHRISTMAS COOKIES

Chocolate-Filled Pecan
Hearts and Stars

Mocha Snowdrops

Coconut Jumbles

Lemon-Sesame Crisps

Cranberry Crunch Cookies

Jam Pinwheels

Spicy Anise Snaps

Having included Christmas in all my books (and even doing an entire book, *The Holidays*, about the end-of-the-year holiday season), I think everyone has at least a faint idea of how much I love Christmastime. And, judging from conversations I've had with readers and from letters I've received, I know that I'm not alone when I say it's my favorite time of year. I've passed along some of my Christmas traditions and you've passed some of yours on to me, so during the holiday season it seems like we're all a big and growing family; I hope we'll think of one another when we sit down at the Christmas table.

I don't have a single traditional Christmas dinner that I serve year after year, but I do always include traditional elements in the menu. This dinner, centered around ducklings roasted the old-world way my Grandma Stapleton always did, is accompanied by a new-world cranberry dressing; there are other old and new world influences as well. After a big Christmas dinner, it's a good idea to take a few hours break before serving dessert, making it almost a separate meal. And that's plenty for one day.

The Christmas Day table is decorated with old-world glass ornaments, ribbons, and greens.

Getting Ready This is a big menu, but a little advance preparation and orchestration, along with some "volunteer" assistance, can make it come together.

The soup, pie, pudding, Rum Custard Sauce, and cookies can be prepared in advance; see the individual recipes for timing.

A day in advance or early in the day, precook the beans and the cabbage, then store in the refrigerator until cooking time. Also early in the day, prepare the dressing and the turnip and potato puree, then cover and refrigerate them. Remember to allow them to come to room temperature before putting them into the oven.

Early in the day, bake the biscuit sticks (or, if you have two ovens, bake them just before serving). Warm them just before serving.

Three hours before dinner, get the ducks ready and begin roasting them and the stuffing.

About an hour before the ducks will come out of the oven, start the caramelized onions and get the steamed pudding ready to be rewarmed.

Have the turnip and potato puree ready to go into the oven as soon as the duck comes out; reduce the heat to 375°F. first.

Start warming the soup 20 minutes before serving. About 15 minutes before serving, start finishing the cabbage, then warm the biscuits for 4 or 5 minutes in the oven. Start warming the steamed pudding as the main course is served.

Serve a California Zinfandel or Pinot Noir with the main course (I'd skip wine with the sherried soup) and, after dessert, one of the berry dessert wines (page 103).

Sherried Butternut Squash and Chestnut Soup

ℒa

SERVES 8 TO 10

This soup has a rich and complex flavor even though it's really not very rich at all.

Next to roasting them, my favorite way to have chestnuts is in this wonderful soup.

2 tablespoons butter
1 medium onion, coarsely chopped
3 shallots, coarsely chopped
2 carrots, sliced
1 stalk celery, coarsely chopped
5 cups chicken stock
1 cup dry sherry
¾ pound chestnuts, peeled (see Note)
    and coarsely chopped
3 pounds butternut squash, peeled and
    coarsely chopped
1 teaspoon grated gingerroot *or*
    ¼ teaspoon ground ginger
3 cups lowfat milk
Salt and white pepper to taste
Snipped chives, for garnish
Grated nutmeg

1. Melt the butter in a Dutch oven or large, heavy saucepan over medium heat. Add the on-ion, shallots, carrots, and celery to the pan and sauté until the onion is golden, 5 to 7 minutes. Add the chicken stock, sherry, chestnuts, squash, and ginger to the pan, raise the heat to medium-high, and bring to a boil. Reduce the heat and simmer until the squash and chestnuts are very tender, about 40 minutes.

2. Remove the pan from the heat and allow to cool slightly. In batches, puree the mixture in the bowl of a food processor fitted with the steel chopping blade, then return the mixture to the pan. Stir in the milk and season to taste with salt and white pepper. *(The soup can be made a day in advance and refrigerated or several weeks in advance and frozen.)*

3. To serve, slowly reheat the soup over low heat, stirring occasionally to prevent sticking. Serve hot, garnished with snipped chives and a grating of nutmeg.

Note: To peel chestnuts, cut Xs into the flat sides using a sharp paring knife. Drop the chestnuts into a pot of boiling water and boil for about 15 minutes. Remove a few at a time and peel off the outer and inner skins. If the skins are too difficult to remove, boil a few minutes longer.

Baking Powder Biscuit Sticks

ℒa

MAKES ABOUT 2 DOZEN

A lot of folks think of biscuits as Southern but we Yankees eat plenty of them, too, for breakfast, lunch, and dinner. If there wasn't so much going on in the oven getting dinner ready, these could be mixed up in a minute or two and baked just before serving, but in this case it's easier to bake them early in the day, then reheat them for a few minutes in a moderate oven.

1¾ cups all-purpose flour
½ teaspoon salt
3 teaspoons double-acting baking powder
⅓ cup chilled vegetable shortening
¾ cup milk

1. Preheat the oven to 450°F. In a mixing bowl, stir together the flour, salt, and baking powder, then cut in the vegetable shortening. Pour the milk into the bowl, then mix until the dry ingredients are just moistened and a soft dough has formed.

2. Turn the dough out onto a lightly floured surface and pat it out to a rectangle about ¼ inch thick. Fold the dough into quarters, then pat it out again to a thickness of ¼ inch; repeat twice.

3. Cut the dough into strips about 3 x ¾ inch and place about 1 inch apart on an ungreased baking sheet. Bake until the biscuits are risen and golden brown, 10 to 12 minutes. Serve hot.

Roasted Ducklings Grandma Stapleton's Way with Wine Gravy

%

SERVES 8

Duck presents one of those cooking problems: A duck is really a little too big to serve two but a little too small to serve four, and as far as I know, no one's quite figured out how to cut one up to evenly serve three. At Christmastime, when everyone seems to have bigger appetites than usual, I allow one duck for every two people. If there's any left over, it becomes lunch the next day, warmed, carved into small slices, and served on a bed of greens with toasted walnuts, sliced apples or pears, and Walnut Dressing (page 169).

This old Czech method of roasting duck, rubbing it with caraway, coarse salt, and pepper, and then roasting it with an orange inside (stuffing was never baked in the bird), is the one my grandmother always used.

4 4- to 5-pound ducklings
3 tablespoons coarse (kosher) salt
3 tablespoons caraway seeds
4 oranges, quartered
4 garlic cloves, peeled and crushed
½ cup orange juice

1 cup dry red wine (see Note)
3 tablespoons cornstarch mixed with
    1 cup cold chicken or duck stock
Salt and coarsely ground black pepper
Pinch of sugar
Lemon leaves and spiced lady apples,
    for garnish

1. Wash the ducks inside and out; dry with paper towels. Using a sharp-tined meat fork, prick the skin all over. Rub the ducks inside and out with the salt and caraway seeds. Place 4 orange quarters and 1 garlic clove into the cavity of each duck.

2. Preheat the oven to 450°F. Arrange the ducks, breast side up, on a rack in a large shallow roasting pan (or 2 roasting pans) and pour the orange juice over them. Roast for 30 minutes and reduce the heat to 400°F. Continue roasting for another hour, then prick the skin all over again with the fork and baste with the pan juices. With the baster, remove most of the fat from the pan, reserving 3 tablespoons fat for the caramelized onions (page 146).

3. Continue roasting for about 45 minutes, basting at 15-minute intervals, or until the duck is a deep, even brown. Remove the ducks to a large platter (I use a turkey platter), cover loosely with foil, and keep warm.

4. To make the gravy, first skim all visible fat from the pan juices. Scrape any browned bits from the bottom and sides of the pan, then transfer the juices to a large measuring cup. Add the wine, place the saucepan over medium-high heat, and bring to a boil. Gradually whisk in the cornstarch mixture and continue cooking until the gravy is slightly thickened. Season to taste with salt, pepper, and a pinch of sugar. Transfer the gravy to a gravy boat or serving bowl.

5. Cut the ducks in half and arrange the halves on a platter. Garnish with lemon leaves and spiced lady apples. Pass the gravy separately.

Note: Chicken or duck stock can be substituted for the wine.

Cranberry-Herb Dressing

ℬ

SERVES 8 TO 10

I don't care much for most duck-with-fruit dishes because they tend to be awfully sweet, but tart cranberries with just a touch of sugar added is a great way to complement crisp roasted duck.

7 cups seeded rye bread cubes
½ cup sugar
½ cup water
2 cups cranberries
1 large onion, coarsely chopped
1 stalk celery, diced
½ cup (1 stick) butter
½ to 1 cup chicken stock or water
Juice and grated rind of 1 orange
¼ cup chopped parsley
½ teaspoon dried thyme
½ teaspoon dried rubbed sage
½ teaspoon ground allspice
½ teaspoon salt
½ teaspoon coarsely ground black pepper
2 large eggs, lightly beaten

1. Preheat the oven to 300°F. Spread the bread cubes in an even layer on a baking sheet and toast until dry and lightly browned, 7 to 10 minutes. Remove from the oven and let cool. (Can be done a day or two in advance.)

2. While the bread is toasting, combine the sugar and water in a medium saucepan and bring to a boil, stirring to dissolve the sugar. Boil about 5 minutes, until the mixture becomes syrupy. Add the cranberries to the pan and let them simmer until the first few berries begin to pop, about 5 minutes. Remove from the heat and drain.

3. In a skillet, sauté the onion and celery in the butter until the onion is golden, 7 to 10 minutes. Transfer to a large mixing bowl, then add the bread cubes, berries, ½ cup chicken stock, and the remaining ingredients. Toss to mix well. Add more chicken stock if the mixture seems dry.

4. Transfer the stuffing to a well-buttered shallow 2½-quart baking dish and cover the dish with its lid or aluminum foil. Place in the oven to bake along with the duck. When the duck is done, the dressing will be done; remove from the oven and keep warm until serving.

Green Beans with Caramelized Onions

ℬ

SERVES 8 TO 10

2 pounds green beans, trimmed
3 tablespoons duck fat, skimmed from the roasting pan (butter can be substituted)
24 small white onions, peeled
2 teaspoons light brown sugar
Coarsely ground black pepper

1. Place the beans in a large kettle with salted water to cover by 2 inches. Place over medium-high heat and cook until just tender, about 15 minutes. Drain the beans and reserve. (The beans can be precooked a day in advance and refrigerated; return to room temperature before finishing.)

2. Place the duck fat in a large Dutch oven and place over medium-high heat until sizzling. Add the onions and reduce the heat to medium-low. Cover the pan loosely and cook, tossing occasionally, until the onions are just tender and a deep, golden brown, 20 to 30 minutes.

3. Sprinkle the sugar and a generous grinding of pepper over the onions and turn carefully. Cook 5 minutes longer, glazing the onions on all sides. (If made with butter, the onions can be made a day in advance and refrigerated.)

4. Add the reserved beans to the onions and toss to combine. Continue cooking until the beans are heated through. Transfer the mixture to a vegetable bowl and serve hot.

The ducks are served with spiced apples on a big turkey platter (opposite, top).

The main course (opposite, bottom) reminds me of old-fashioned Christmas dinners at my grandmother's house.

CHRISTMAS MEMORIES

Probably the happiest Christmas memories for all of us are of the Christmases of our childhoods. I remember waking up on Christmas mornings and hearing my father outside opening the barn doors to feed the animals and hearing my mother and grandmother downstairs in the kitchen preparing the food for the day. And already I could smell the turkey roasting. We kids weren't allowed downstairs until Dad came back inside from his morning chores and I think those were the longest waits in my life, because I knew that once the day began it would offer one thrill after another.

We never had Christmas stockings, but instead each of us received a tin filled with fudge, cookies, and fruits. In those days in the country, fresh fruit in winter was not widely available, so an orange was just as prized to me as the latest electronic toy is to a kid nowadays. Each of us kids received only two or three small gifts, but we always considered each gift very special, and ourselves very lucky. And when dinnertime came, we always thought it was the best dinner we'd ever had.

Today, Christmas for me is a day of gathering to share family stories and news, watching the kids play with their toys, listening to carols, and enjoying a wonderful dinner together. But the smell of an orange being peeled, or dinner roasting in the oven, or the sound of a few notes of a certain carol always sends me back to our old farmhouse and I can hear Mom and Grandma down in the kitchen and Dad coming in from outside. And we four kids are perched at the top of the steps just waiting for Christmas Day to begin.

Even if you can't go home again, the memories sure can.

Bohemian Creamed Cabbage

§a

SERVES 8

In Eastern Europe, cabbage is a traditional accompaniment to duck. As a hot vegetable, cabbage has earned a rather stinky reputation from being boiled to death in too many pots of corned beef and cabbage. This version of an old family recipe makes the unfairly maligned cabbage into a tasty side dish.

1 medium head cabbage, cut into ¼-inch shreds
3 tablespoons butter
6 scallions, white and green parts, chopped
1 cup light cream
⅛ teaspoon grated nutmeg
⅛ teaspoon ground mild paprika
⅛ teaspoon finely ground black pepper

1. In a large pan, cover the cabbage with salted water. Place over medium-high heat and bring to a simmer. Reduce the heat to low and simmer the cabbage until just tender, about 8 minutes. Drain the cabbage. (*The cabbage can be made up to a day in advance to this point and refrigerated.*)

2. Melt the butter in a large skillet over medium heat. Add the scallions and sauté 5 minutes. Add the cabbage to the pan along with the cream, nutmeg, paprika, and pepper. Toss well to mix all the ingredients. Cook, stirring constantly, until the cream thickens and the cabbage is hot, about 5 minutes. Serve hot.

Baked Turnip and Potato Puree

§a

SERVES 8 TO 10

Even people who turn up their noses at the mention of turnips will like this soufflélike baked puree. It's delicious either all by itself or topped with a little duck gravy.

1½ pounds white turnips, cooked and mashed
1½ pounds potatoes, cooked and mashed
⅓ cup (⅔ stick) butter, melted
1 teaspoon sugar

¼ teaspoon salt
¼ teaspoon white pepper
3 large eggs, well beaten

1. Preheat the oven to 375°F. Lightly grease a shallow 2-quart baking dish.

2. In a mixing bowl, combine all the ingredients and mix well. Mound the mixture into the prepared baking dish, leaving the surface "hilly." *(The puree can be made several hours in advance up to this point. Cover tightly and refrigerate, then bring to room temperature before proceeding.)* Bake until the top is slightly puffed and nicely browned, about 30 minutes.

Steamed Banana, Date, and Pineapple Pudding

✇

SERVES 8

It's no secret that I'm a big fan of steamed puddings and Christmastime is as good a time as any for old-fashioned desserts. I wouldn't go quite so far as to call this one light, but it is a far less rich alternative to the usual plum pudding.

1 cup chopped dates
2 cups all-purpose flour
1¼ cups sugar
1 teaspoon baking powder
½ teaspoon baking soda
¼ teaspoon salt
½ teaspoon ground cinnamon
½ teaspoon ground ginger
¼ teaspoon grated nutmeg
2 cups mashed very ripe bananas
2 tablespoons molasses
¼ cup butter, melted
¼ cup milk
1 large egg
1 9-ounce can crushed pineapple in juice, drained

1. Toss the dates with 2 tablespoons flour and reserve. In a large mixing bowl, sift together the remaining flour, sugar, baking powder, baking soda, salt, and spices. In a separate bowl, combine the bananas, molasses, butter, milk, and egg and mix well. Gradually beat the dry ingredients into the wet mixture, beating until well blended and smooth. Stir in the floured dates and the pineapple.

2. Lightly butter a 6-cup pudding mold or deep baking dish. Transfer the batter to the mold and cover tightly with its lid or with aluminum foil. Place the mold in a large kettle and pour boiling water into the kettle to come ⅔ of the way up the sides of the mold. Cover the kettle, place over low heat, and steam for 2¼ hours.

3. Remove the mold from the kettle and allow the pudding to cool for an hour before serving. *(The pudding can be made up to two days in advance and stored, in the mold, in the refrigerator; allow to come to room temperature, then reheat by steaming for 45 minutes.)* Slice the pudding and serve it warm with Rum Custard Sauce.

Rum Custard Sauce

✇

MAKES ABOUT 2 CUPS

1 cup milk
4 large egg yolks, at room temperature
3 tablespoons sugar
2 tablespoons light rum
1 teaspoon vanilla extract

1. In a small saucepan, scald the milk, remove from the heat, and set aside.

2. In the top of a double boiler not yet over the heat, whisk the egg yolks and sugar together until thick and lemon colored. Gradually whisk in the milk and the rum. Place over simmering water and cook, whisking constantly, until the custard is thick enough to coat a spoon thickly, about 10 minutes.

3. Remove the pan from the heat and stir in the vanilla. Transfer the sauce to a small bowl, place a piece of plastic wrap directly onto the surface of the sauce to prevent a skin from forming, cool, and chill thoroughly. *(Can be made up to two days in advance.)*

BOXWOOD CHRISTMAS "TREE"

To make the tree on the sideboard, push 6- to 8-inch sprigs of freshly cut boxwood into a styrofoam cone to cover it completely. Place the tree in a decorative bowl, then decorate it with a string of tiny white lights. Wire on sprigs of holly, hydrangea blossoms, winterberries, raffia, small gold Christmas tree balls, and loops of wired gold ribbon. The tree will last a week or more.

Hazelnut Fudge Pie

ℒ

MAKES ONE 9-INCH PIE

The filling of this pie has a rich, soft, brownie-like texture. Try a thin slice topped with a small scoop of Vanilla Ice Cream (page 58) or Rum Custard Sauce (page 149).

Basic Pastry (page 85)
3 squares unsweetened chocolate, coarsely chopped
¾ cup (1½ sticks) butter
3 large eggs, lightly beaten
1½ cups sugar
¼ teaspoon salt
⅓ cup all-purpose flour
1 teaspoon vanilla extract
1½ cups chopped hazelnuts, lightly toasted
Confectioners' sugar, for dusting

1. Preheat the oven to 450°F. Line a 9-inch pie pan with the pastry, prick well with a fork, and crimp the edges.

2. Meanwhile, in the top of a double boiler over simmering water (or in a medium, heavy saucepan over very low heat), combine the chocolate and butter and stir until melted and blended. Remove the pan from the heat and allow to cool.

3. Using a large spoon, beat the eggs into the

Dessert is served on the sideboard alongside a lit and decorated boxwood "tree."

pan. Gradually beat in the sugar and salt, and then the flour. Stir in the vanilla and nuts. Transfer this batter to the prebaked pastry shell.

4. Bake for 10 minutes, then turn the heat down to 325°F. Continue baking until the filling is set, about 40 minutes. Place the pie on a rack to cool. Serve warm or at room temperature, dusted lightly with confectioners' sugar.

Chocolate-Filled Pecan Hearts and Stars

ℒ

MAKES ABOUT 2 DOZEN, DEPENDING ON THE SIZE OF THE CUTTERS

1 cup (2 sticks) butter
⅔ cup confectioners' sugar
2 cups all-purpose flour
¾ cup finely ground pecans
1½ teaspoons vanilla extract
⅛ teaspoon salt
Confectioners' sugar, for dusting
4 ounces (4 squares) semisweet chocolate, melted and cooled

1. Preheat the oven to 325°F. Lightly grease baking sheets or line them with parchment.

2. In a mixing bowl, cream the butter and sugar together, then mix in the flour and pecans. Add the vanilla and salt and mix well. Form the dough into a ball and flatten slightly. Cover with plastic wrap and chill 2 hours.

3. On a lightly floured surface, roll out the dough to a thickness of ⅛ inch. Using floured small cutters, cut out even numbers of hearts and stars. Place on the baking sheets about 1 inch apart and bake until very lightly browned, about 5 to 7 minutes. Transfer to wire racks to cool. While still slightly warm, dust the cookies generously with confectioners' sugar.

4. Thinly spread the flat undersides of half the cookies with melted chocolate, then back with another cookie, pressing lightly to adhere. Pack the cookies in tightly covered containers and store in a cool place.

Mocha Snowdrops

❧

MAKES ABOUT 6 DOZEN

1 cup (2 sticks) butter, softened
½ cup sugar
2 teaspoons vanilla extract
1¾ cups all-purpose flour
½ teaspoon salt
½ teaspoon ground cinnamon
2 teaspoons instant coffee powder
    (not granules)
¼ cup unsweetened cocoa
2 cups finely chopped walnuts
Confectioners' sugar, for dusting

1. Preheat the oven to 350°F. Lightly grease baking sheets or line them with parchment.

2. In a mixing bowl, cream the butter and sugar together until light and fluffy, then beat in the vanilla. In a separate bowl, sift together the flour, salt, cinnamon, coffee, and cocoa, then beat the dry ingredients into the wet mixture, forming a soft dough. Beat in the nuts.

3. Roll the dough into balls about ¾ inch in diameter and place on the baking sheets about 1 inch apart. Bake until the cookies are lightly browned, 10 to 12 minutes, and remove to wire racks to cool. Roll the cookies in confectioners' sugar to coat them well, then pack into tightly covered containers and store in a cool place.

Coconut Jumbles

❧

MAKES ABOUT 6 DOZEN COOKIES

I found this recipe on a yellowed 3 x 5 card that was in an old recipe box I bought at a tag sale. The recipe, written in an old-fashioned hand, was rather vague, but I figured it out.

¾ cup (1½ sticks) butter, softened
1 cup sugar
2 large eggs
1 teaspoon vanilla extract
1 teaspoon almond extract
2 cups all-purpose flour
½ teaspoon salt
½ teaspoon baking soda
¼ cup sour cream
1½ cups chopped walnuts
2 cups shredded coconut
1½ cups golden raisins

1. Preheat the oven to 375°F. Lightly grease baking sheets or line them with parchment.

2. In a mixing bowl, cream the butter and sugar together until light and fluffy, then beat in the eggs, vanilla, and almond extract. Gradually beat the flour and salt into the wet mixture. In a separate small bowl, stir the baking soda and sour cream together. Beat the sour cream mixture into the larger bowl, then stir in the walnuts, coconut, and raisins.

3. Drop the dough by teaspoonfuls onto the baking sheets about 2 inches apart. Bake until lightly browned, about 10 minutes, and remove to wire racks to cool. Pack into tightly covered containers and store in a cool place.

Lemon – Sesame Crisps

❧

MAKES ABOUT 6 DOZEN COOKIES

½ cup (1 stick) butter, softened
½ cup vegetable shortening
1 cup sugar
1 large egg
1 teaspoon vanilla extract
Grated rind of 1 lemon
2 cups all-purpose flour
½ teaspoon baking soda
½ teaspoon salt
½ cup sesame seeds

1. Cream the butter, shortening, and sugar together until light and fluffy, then beat in the egg, the vanilla, and lemon rind. In a separate bowl, sift the flour, baking soda, and salt together, then gradually beat the dry ingredients into the wet mixture, forming a soft dough. Form the dough into a ball, wrap with waxed paper or plastic wrap, and chill 2 hours.

I bake lots of Christmas cookies to have on Christmas Day and all through the season.

2. Preheat the oven to 350°F. Lightly grease baking sheets or line them with parchment.

3. Pour the sesame seeds into a shallow bowl. A teaspoonful at a time, form the dough into small balls, then roll the balls in the sesame seeds to coat them well. Place the balls about 2 inches apart on the baking sheets and bake until the edges of the cookies are lightly browned, 8 to 10 minutes. Remove the cookies to wire racks to cool, then store in tightly covered containers in a cool place.

Cranberry Crunch Cookies

ళు

MAKES ABOUT 6 DOZEN COOKIES

Dried cranberries give these cookies chewiness, while cornmeal and nuts add crunch.

2¼ cups sugar
½ cup vegetable shortening
1¼ cups (2½ sticks) butter, softened
3 large eggs

1½ cups stone-ground yellow cornmeal
3½ cups all-purpose flour
1 teaspoon baking powder
½ teaspoon salt
½ teaspoon ground cinnamon
½ teaspoon ground cloves
¼ teaspoon grated nutmeg
1½ cups dried cranberries
1½ cups chopped pecans

1. Preheat the oven to 375°F. Lightly grease baking sheets or line them with parchment.

2. In a mixing bowl, cream the sugar, shortening, and butter together until light and fluffy, then beat in the eggs. In a separate bowl, sift together the cornmeal, flour, baking powder, salt, and spices. Beat the dry mixture into the wet mixture, then stir in the cranberries and nuts.

3. Drop dough by the heaping teaspoonful about 2 inches apart onto the prepared baking sheets. Bake until the edges are lightly browned, about 10 minutes. Transfer the cookies to wire racks to cool, then store in tightly covered containers.

Jam Pinwheels

❧

First off, you need to start these cookies two days before you want to serve them. These are a little more complicated than most cookies, but I make all kinds of once-a-year exceptions at Christmastime, especially when the end results look and taste as Christmasy as these cookies do. I usually make a double batch.

- ½ cup (1 stick) butter, softened
- ¾ cup sugar
- 1 large egg
- ½ teaspoon vanilla extract
- ½ teaspoon almond extract
- 2 cups all-purpose flour
- ½ teaspoon baking powder
- ¼ teaspoon salt
- ¼ teaspoon grated nutmeg
- ¼ teaspoon ground cinnamon
- ½ cup ground blanched almonds
- ½ cup strawberry jam or seedless raspberry jam

1. In a mixing bowl, cream the butter and sugar together until light and fluffy, then beat in the egg, vanilla, and almond extract. In a separate bowl, sift together the flour, baking powder, salt, and spices. Beat the dry mixture into the wet mixture, forming a soft dough. Form the dough into a ball, wrap in wax paper or plastic wrap, and refrigerate 6 hours or overnight.

2. In a small bowl, combine the almonds and jam, mix well, and set aside. On a lightly floured work surface, roll out the dough into a rectangle about 12 x 15 inches. Spread the jam mixture evenly over the dough. With the long side of the dough facing you, carefully roll the dough away from you, rolling it up like a jelly roll. Wrap the dough roll and refrigerate overnight.

3. Preheat the oven to 350°F. Lightly grease baking sheets or line them with parchment.

4. Using a sharp knife, cut the dough roll into ¼-inch thick slices. Place the slices 2 inches apart on the baking sheets and bake until very lightly browned on the edges, about 10 minutes. Remove the cookies to wire racks to cool, then transfer to tightly sealed containers and store in a cool place.

Marmalade Pinwheels Substitute a good-quality thin-cut orange marmalade for the jam.

Spicy Anise Snaps

❧

Anise seeds add a little surprise to these cookies that look just like gingersnaps.

- ⅔ cup (1⅓ sticks) butter, softened
- 1 cup firmly packed dark brown sugar
- 1 large egg
- 2 tablespoons molasses
- ½ teaspoon vanilla extract
- 2¼ cups all-purpose flour
- 1½ teaspoons baking soda
- ½ teaspoon salt
- ½ teaspoon ground ginger
- ½ teaspoon ground cinnamon
- ¼ teaspoon ground cloves
- ¼ teaspoon finely ground black pepper
- 1 teaspoon anise seeds
- Granulated sugar

1. In a mixing bowl, cream the butter and brown sugar together until light and fluffy. Beat in the egg and then the molasses and vanilla. In a separate bowl, sift together the flour, baking soda, salt, and spices. Gradually beat the dry ingredients and the anise seeds into the wet mixture, forming a soft dough. Form the dough into a ball and flatten slightly. Wrap in wax paper or plastic wrap and refrigerate 2 hours.

2. Preheat the oven to 350°F. Lightly grease baking sheets. Shape the dough into small balls about ¾ inch in diameter and roll the balls in granulated sugar, coating them well. Place the balls 2 inches apart on the baking sheets and bake until the edges are browned, 10 to 12 minutes. Transfer the cookies onto wire racks to cool, then store in a cool place.

VANOCHKA FOR
CHRISTMAS DAY BREAKFAST

Over the years I have simplified my Christmas day schedule; I don't plan too much to eat during the day when there's an early big dinner on the way. For a late breakfast I usually bake a traditional German stollen (the recipe appears in *The Holidays*) or the traditional Bohemian Vanochka, a braided, lightly spiced bread studded with fruits, and serve it with coffee and an assortment of fresh fruit. I serve Vanochka for breakfast, but in the old country it's traditionally served to roving carolers with a glass of wine.

1 envelope active dry yeast
¼ cup warm water
¼ cup butter
½ cup sugar
2 large eggs
5 to 6 cups all-purpose flour
1½ teaspoons salt
¼ teaspoon ground cardamom
1 cup warm milk
Grated rind of 1 lemon
½ cup golden raisins
½ cup chopped candied orange peel
½ cup chopped citron
½ cup chopped almonds, lightly toasted
1 large egg yolk, lightly beaten with
    1 tablespoon milk
¼ cup sliced almonds
Sugar, for sprinkling

1. Pour the warm water into a small bowl, then sprinkle the yeast over it and stir to dissolve. Set aside.

2. In a large mixing bowl, cream the butter and ½ cup sugar together until light and fluffy, then beat in the eggs, one at a time. Beat in 1 cup of the flour, along with the salt and cardamom. Beat in the milk, the yeast mixture, and the lemon peel. A cup at a time, beat in additional flour until a very soft dough forms. Then beat in the raisins, candied fruit, and chopped almonds.

3. Turn the dough out onto a well-floured work surface and, ½ cup at a time, knead additional flour into the dough until it is satiny and elastic. Form the dough into a ball and place in an oiled bowl. Cover with a clean towel and allow the dough to rise until doubled in bulk, 1 to 1½ hours.

4. Punch the dough down and divide it into 4 equal portions. Set one portion aside and roll the remaining 3 parts into a cylinder about 1¼ inches in diameter. Lay the 3 cylinders side by side lengthwise on a lightly greased baking sheet and braid them, sealing the ends by brushing the dough with water.

5. Divide the reserved dough into 3 equal portions and roll into cylinders about ¾ inch in diameter. On the work surface, braid the 3 cylinders and seal the ends as above. Brush the surface of the large braid lightly with water and center the small braid on top of it. Cover loosely with the towel and let rise until double in bulk, about 45 minutes.

6. Preheat the oven to 350°F. Brush the surface of the dough with the beaten egg mixture, scatter the sliced almonds over the surface, then sprinkle generously with sugar. Bake until the bread sounds hollow when tapped with a finger and is golden brown, 35 to 40 minutes. Remove to a wire rack to cool. Serve warm or at room temperature, sliced, with sweet butter.

A Holiday Tasting Party

FOR 25

℘

MENU

Mulled Cranberry
Madras Punch

• • •

"City Chicken" with
Apple Ketchup (page 159)

Chicken Liver Spread with
Currants and Port

Cheese and Mushroom Turnovers

Pickled Shrimp

Blanched Green Vegetables with
Roasted Red Pepper Sauce

Aunt Bertie's Ham Balls

"Hot-as-Hades" Pepper Jam
(page 100) and Cream Cheese on
Caraway Black Bread (page 38)

Spiced Pumpkin Butter
(page 97) on Nut Brown Bread

• • •

Apricot-Coconut Tartlets

Lemon Bars

Chocolate Chip Oatmeal Squares

**Wreaths and candles at the windows and
a spotlight on the front door send a message
of welcome and good cheer (above).**

I have a big open house party every winter, traditionally at holiday time. When I lived in the city the party was always on New Year's Day and there was always a crowd. Last year was my first year in the country, so I moved the party to the weekend between Christmas and New Year's. I really didn't expect a lot of people to trek out from the city, but when the party began, all the regulars started drifting in; in fact, many of my old friends arrived ahead of my new and nearby neighbors.

Because it's a large party I always serve finger foods so everyone can have plenty to eat even if they can't get to a seat. And I make the food pretty substantial so it can serve as a meal.

Getting Ready Make sure all serving dishes are ready and list what each item will be served on. Plan how the buffet will be arranged in advance and allow a half hour before the guests arrive to get everything organized.

The Apple Ketchup can be made well in advance. The breads and pastry dough for the turnovers, too, can be made in advance and frozen (or make the breads a day before the party).

All the sweets can be made a day in advance. Also on the day before the party, make the shrimp, the ham balls, and red pepper sauce, and assemble the turnovers.

Either the night before (no sooner) or early on the day of the party (no later), make the chicken liver spread and the city chicken. Blanch the vegetables anytime during the day.

Inside, the tree and mantel are decorated and everything's lit up and ready for company.

Start the punch an hour or so before the beginning of the party.

Bake the turnovers and reheat the ham balls just before serving.

This is a variety of tastes, so the usual "serve this wine with this" rules don't apply. In addition to the punch I offer a variety of wines, usually two whites and one red. And there's always a pot of coffee available.

Mulled Cranberry Madras Punch

ℰℬ

MAKES THIRTY-TWO
6-OUNCE DRINKS

Here's a mild punch that can be served either warm or on ice. If you'd like something a bit stronger, try adding a dash of rum to each serving, either way.

- 3 quarts cranberry juice cocktail
- 1 quart orange juice
- 4 3- to 4-inch cinnamon sticks
- 1 teaspoon whole allspice
- 1 teaspoon whole cloves
- 1 medium orange, thinly sliced
- ½ gallon dry white wine

Combine the cranberry juice, orange juice, spices, and orange slices in a large kettle and place over low heat. Bring the mixture to the simmering point, then reduce the heat to very low and allow the mixture to steep for 1 hour. Stir in the wine, bring to just below the simmering point, and keep warm for serving.

"City Chicken" with Apple Ketchup

ℰℬ

MAKES ABOUT 40
HORS D'OEUVRES

No, this isn't chicken at all. It's an old recipe from the days when "a chicken in every pot" was an expensive delicacy, a luxury for city folks far away from the farm. So cubes of pork and veal, far less expensive meats at the time, were "disguised" as the more luxurious bird.

- ⅔ cup flour
- 3 large eggs, lightly beaten
- 2 cups fine cracker crumbs
- ½ teaspoon salt
- ½ teaspoon finely ground black pepper
- ½ teaspoon dried rubbed sage
- ½ teaspoon dried thyme
- 1 teaspoon mild paprika
- 2 tablespoons finely chopped parsley
- 2 pounds boneless pork, cut into ¾-inch chunks
- 2 pounds boneless veal, cut into ¾-inch chunks
- About 40 6-inch bamboo skewers
- Vegetable shortening
- 1½ cups well-seasoned chicken stock, approximately
- Apple Ketchup (page 100), for dipping

1. Place the flour in a shallow bowl, the eggs in a second shallow bowl, and combine the cracker crumbs, salt, and seasonings in a third shallow bowl. Skewer the meat, alternating 2 cubes each of the pork and veal, compactly onto the bamboo skewers. Roll the meat in the flour, then in the beaten egg, and lastly in the seasoned crumbs. Let stand 30 minutes.

2. In a large skillet over medium heat, melt enough vegetable shortening to cover the bottom of the skillet and heat until sizzling. A few skewers at a time, brown the meat on all sides, then arrange in a single layer in a large shallow baking pan, or 2 pans if necessary.

3. Preheat the oven to 375°F. Pour enough stock into the pan(s) to reach a depth of ¼ inch. Cover the pan(s) loosely with aluminum foil and bake until the meat is tender, turning once, about 20 minutes. *(Can be made up to a day in advance, covered, and refrigerated. Reheat in a 350°F. oven for 10 to 15 minutes.)*

I love cranberries any way, and here's my cranberry-based holiday punch (opposite).

Chicken Liver Spread with Currants and Port

ℰ

MAKES 4 CUPS

Serve this with quartered slices of thinly sliced Caraway Black Bread (page 38) or store-bought pumpernickel or rye.

¾ cup dried currants
⅓ cup Port or cognac
¼ cup (½ stick) butter
3 large garlic cloves, chopped
1 medium onion, coarsely chopped
2 pounds chicken livers
¾ teaspoon salt
⅛ teaspoon cayenne pepper
⅛ teaspoon freshly ground black pepper
¼ teaspoon grated nutmeg
¼ teaspoon ground cloves
½ cup (1 stick) butter, softened

1. In a small, heavy saucepan, combine the currants and Port. Place over medium heat and bring to a simmer. Remove from the heat and let stand 1 hour to plump the currants.

2. In a large, heavy skillet, melt ¼ cup butter over medium heat. Add the garlic and onion and sauté until nicely browned, about 15 minutes. Add the chicken livers and sauté until brown on the outside but still slightly pink on the inside, 5 to 7 minutes.

3. Transfer the mixture to the bowl of a food processor fitted with the steel chopping blade. Add the salt, peppers, nutmeg, cloves, and softened butter and process until the mixture is smooth.

4. Transfer the mixture to a mixing bowl and stir in the currants and port. Cover with plastic wrap, pressing the wrap directly onto the mixture, and refrigerate 6 hours or overnight to allow the flavors to blend. Bring to room temperature before serving.

Cheese and Mushroom Turnovers

ℰ

MAKES ABOUT 4 DOZEN

1 tablespoon butter
4 scallions, white and green parts, finely chopped
1 cup finely chopped button mushrooms
2 teaspoons all-purpose flour
⅓ cup milk
1 cup grated Swiss cheese
¼ cup grated Parmesan cheese
⅛ teaspoon dry mustard
⅛ teaspoon grated nutmeg
⅛ teaspoon salt
⅛ teaspoon finely ground black pepper
Double recipe Basic Pastry (page 85)
1 large egg, lightly beaten with
    1 tablespoon milk

1. In a medium skillet, melt the butter over medium heat. Add the scallions and mushrooms and sauté until the mushrooms are browned and their juices hve evaporated, 7 to 10 minutes. Gradually add the flour, stirring until blended in. Gradually stir in the milk and continue cooking until the mixture is thickened and smooth, 2 to 3 minutes. Remove from the heat and allow to cool, then stir in the cheeses, mustard, nutmeg, salt, and pepper. Set aside.

2. Roll out the pastry to a thickness of ⅛ inch. Using a 3-inch biscuit cutter, cut circles from the pastry. Place 1 teaspoon of the cheese mixture onto each pastry circle, slightly off center. Moisten the pastry edges with water, fold the circles in half over the filling, and press to seal the edges completely. *(The turnovers can be prepared several hours in advance and refrigerated, or well in advance and frozen.)*

3. Preheat the oven to 350°F. Arrange the turnovers on lightly greased baking sheets. Brush the pastry with the beaten egg mixture and bake until golden brown, 25 to 30 minutes. Serve hot.

All my friends have at least a few favorites, so I like to offer a wide variety of tastes.

Pickled Shrimp

MAKES 20 TO 30 PIECES

No matter how much shrimp I make, it always disappears. So my advice is to multiply this recipe as you see fit.

Dressing

¾ cup olive oil

¾ cup vegetable oil

1 cup red wine vinegar

2 tablespoons sugar

1 teaspoon salt

¼ cup tomato paste

1 teaspoon dry mustard

½ teaspoon hot pepper sauce

½ teaspoon red pepper flakes

1 tablespoon black peppercorns

2 tablespoons celery seeds

3 large garlic cloves, crushed

...

4 pounds large shrimp, cooked and peeled

6 bay leaves

1 large onion, thinly sliced and separated into rings

1 small head lettuce

Bamboo skewers

1. In a jar, combine all the dressing ingredients, cover, and shake well. Set aside.

2. Place the shrimp, bay leaves, and onion rings in a large bowl. Add the dressing and toss well to combine the ingredients and coat them with the dressing. Cover tightly and chill for 24 hours, tossing 3 or 4 times.

3. To serve, line a shallow bowl with lettuce leaves. Drain the shrimp mixture and arrange on the lettuce. Serve with toothpicks or bamboo skewers for skewering.

Roasted Red Pepper Sauce

⅌

MAKES 3½ CUPS

A flavorful dipping sauce for any available green vegetables, such as green beans, broccoli spears, asparagus, zucchini sticks, Brussels sprouts, and sugar snap peas. When serving cold vegetables with a dipping sauce, I blanch them for a minute or two first to brighten the color and take the edge off the raw flavor.

4 large red peppers, roasted, seeded, and peeled *or* two 7-ounce jars roasted red peppers, drained
2 large garlic cloves
1½ cups mayonnaise (made with all olive oil and lemon juice)
¼ teaspoon cayenne pepper
1½ teaspoons Dijon mustard
2 teaspoons capers, drained

1. In the bowl of a food processor fitted with the steel chopping blade, combine all ingredients except the capers and process until smooth. Stir in the capers and transfer the mixture to a

small serving bowl. Cover and refrigerate 6 hours or overnight to allow the flavors to blend.

2. To serve, place the bowl on a serving platter and surround with vegetables for dipping.

Aunt Bertie's Ham Balls

⅌

MAKES ABOUT 6 DOZEN

I first tasted ham balls when we once visited Mom's Aunt Bertie. In my seven-year-old opinion, she was quite an elegant lady, since she lived in the big city (Cleveland), had a baby grand piano (ours was only an upright), and served "fancy" foods like this. I've had ham balls many times since, at potlucks and such, but (even though I never had her recipe) ham balls always remind me of going to Aunt Bertie's.

1 pound ground country ham
1 pound lean ground pork
2 large eggs
¼ cup orange juice
1 small onion, chopped
1 small green bell pepper, chopped
1 cup fine cracker crumbs
2 large eggs, lightly beaten
1 teaspoon dry mustard
⅛ teaspoon ground cayenne pepper

Sauce
1 cup orange marmalade
1 cup apple jelly
4 tablespoons dry mustard
6 tablespoons prepared horseradish
½ cup red wine vinegar
¼ teaspoon ground cayenne

1. Preheat the oven to 375° F.

2. In a large bowl, combine all the ingredients for the ham balls and, using your hands, mix well. Form the meat mixture into balls about 1 inch in diameter. Arrange the balls about 1 inch apart on a baking sheet. Bake 15 minutes, turn once, and bake 10 minutes longer. Transfer to absorbent paper to drain any fatty juices.

WINTER "BOUQUETS"

- A wooden bowl filled with lemons and limes
- Bare tree twigs in a colorful porcelain vase
- A big glass vase with branches of evergreens, bitterberries, and holly
- An old earthenware bowl filled with pinecones
- A basket of oranges, sprigs of evergreen, and cinnamon sticks
- Dried flowers arranged together in big bunches rather than piece by piece
- Several white poinsettia plants grouped together in a big basket
- Forced bulbs in a shallow terra-cotta bowl

The mantel is decorated with Santas, greens, grapevines, heather, hydrangeas, and holly.

3. Combine the sauce ingredients in a shallow baking dish and stir well. Add the ham balls and toss to coat with the sauce. Allow to cool, cover tightly, and refrigerate overnight; bring to room temperature before proceeding.

4. Preheat the oven to 350°F. Bake until the sauce is bubbly and the ham balls are heated through, about 30 minutes. Serve from the baking dish with toothpicks or bamboo skewers.

Nut Brown Bread

୬ଥ

MAKES TWO 8½ X 4½-INCH
LOAVES

Slice this bread into ¼-inch slices, then cut the slices in half. Serve with a crock of Spiced Pumpkin Butter (page 97). This bread is best made a day in advance and wrapped well to allow flavors to develop.

  2 cups all-purpose flour
  ½ cup whole wheat flour
  ½ cup stone-ground yellow cornmeal
  ½ cup firmly packed dark brown sugar

  1 tablespoon baking powder
  1 teaspoon salt
  1 large egg
  3 tablespoons butter, melted and cooled
  1½ cups milk
  1 cup chopped walnuts or pecans, lightly
    toasted
  ⅔ cup raisins

1. Preheat the oven to 350°F. Lightly grease two 8½ x 4½-inch loaf pans.

2. In a mixing bowl, combine the flours, cornmeal, brown sugar, baking powder, and salt. In a separate bowl, combine the egg, butter, and milk and stir with a fork until well blended. Add the liquid mixture to the dry ingredients and beat until smooth, then stir in the nuts and raisins.

3. Divide the batter between the pans and bake until the bread is nicely browned and a toothpick or cake tester inserted in the center comes out clean, 35 to 40 minutes. Remove the loaves from the pan and transfer to wire racks to cool completely before slicing. (*The bread can be made several weeks in advance and frozen, tightly wrapped.*)

All my Santas don't fit on the mantel any more, so now I pack them onto the sideboard, too.

Apricot-Coconut Tartlets

ℬ

MAKES 2 DOZEN

¾ cup chopped dried apricots
½ cup water
¼ cup (½ stick) butter, softened
½ cup sugar
2 large eggs
½ teaspoon vanilla extract
¼ cup all-purpose flour
¼ teaspoon baking powder
1 teaspoon grated lemon rind
1½ cups shredded coconut
Double recipe Cream Cheese Pastry
(page 86)

1. In a small saucepan, combine the apricots and water. Place over medium heat and bring to a simmer. Reduce the heat to low, cover the pan loosely, and simmer until the water is absorbed and the apricots are plump and tender, 8 to 10 minutes. Remove from the heat and allow to cool.

2. In a mixing bowl, cream the butter and sugar together, then beat in the eggs and vanilla. Add the flour and baking powder and beat well, then stir in the lemon rind, coconut, and apricots.

3. Preheat the oven to 375°F. Lightly grease two 12-cup miniature muffin pans. Roll out the pastry to a thickness of ⅛ inch and, using a 3-inch biscuit cutter, cut out small circles of dough. Line the muffin cups with the dough, then spoon the apricot-coconut mixture into the cups.

4. Bake until the filling is set and puffs up and the surface is nicely browned, about 20 minutes. Allow the tartlets to cool 10 minutes in the pans, then remove to wire racks to cool completely. *(The tartlets can be made up to a day in advance and stored in air tight containers in a cool place.)*

Lemon Bars

ℬ

MAKES 48

This is one of the best sweets I know, to serve at a party or to have as an afternoon snack with a cup of hot tea.

Crust
1 cup (2 sticks) chilled butter
2 cups all-purpose flour
½ cup sifted confectioners' sugar

Filling

4 large eggs
2 cups sugar
4 tablespoons all-purpose flour
½ teaspoon baking powder
Juice and grated rind of 2 lemons
Confectioners' sugar, for dusting

1. Cut the butter into chunks and place in the bowl of a food processor fitted with the steel chopping blade. Add the flour and sugar, and process, pulsing off and on, until a dough ball forms. Remove the dough, wrap it tightly with wax paper or plastic wrap, and refrigerate it until firm, about 1 hour.

2. Preheat the oven to 325°F. Lightly grease a shallow 9 x 13-inch baking pan. Remove the dough from the refrigerator and press it into an even layer in the bottom of the pan. Bake for 15 minutes, then remove the pan to a wire rack to cool.

3. To prepare the filling, place the eggs in a bowl and beat them until they thicken and lighten in color. Beat in the sugar and then the flour and baking powder. Beat in the lemon juice and rind.

4. Pour the filling mixture evenly over the crust. Place the pan in the oven and bake for 20 minutes longer, or until the filling is set and golden. Remove to a wire rack to cool.

5. Dust the confectioners' sugar over the surface to cover. Cut into 2¼-inch squares, then cut each square diagonally in half to make triangles.

Chocolate Chip Oatmeal Squares

℘

MAKES 36 SQUARES

1 cup (2 sticks) butter
⅓ cup brown sugar
½ cup granulated sugar
1 large egg
1 teaspoon vanilla extract
1¼ cups all-purpose flour

A few sweet treats round out the party.

2¼ cups quick-cooking oatmeal
½ teaspoon salt
1 cup semisweet chocolate chips
½ cup chopped walnuts or pecans

1. Preheat the oven to 350°F. Lightly grease a 9-inch square baking pan.

2. In a mixing bowl, cream the butter and sugars together until light and fluffy, then beat in the egg and the vanilla. Add ¾ of the flour, oatmeal, and salt and beat until blended. Press ¾ of this dough evenly into the prepared pan, then scatter the chocolate chips over the dough. Combine the nuts with the remaining flour and dough and crumble over the chocolate chips.

3. Bake until the edges are browned and a cake tester or toothpick inserted in the center comes out clean, 30 to 35 minutes. Remove the pan to a wire rack to cool, then cut into thirty-six 1½-inch squares. Pack into tightly covered containers and store in a cool place.

Sunday Chicken Dinner

FOR 6

ℰ

MENU

Pam's Chicken Fricassee with
Wild Mushrooms and Sage

Steamed Parsley Dumplings

Cabbage and Carrot Salad with
Walnut Dressing

• • •

Pear-Berry Crisp

Recently my old friend Pam Thomas, a fellow Ohioan and author of several cookbooks herself, invited me to her Manhattan apartment for Sunday dinner with a few other friends. When I arrived, I got a wonderful herby whiff from the kitchen, and I knew right away that we were in for something good. And when we all sat down at the old round oak table in Pam's kitchen, my guess proved to be right. Dinner started with Pam's version of old-fashioned chicken fricassee and dumplings, a favorite dish from long ago that I had forgotten about, and for dessert, a plain and simple spicy Pear Crisp. What a nice way to end the weekend!

Getting Ready Start the fricassee about an hour and a half before serving, or make it a day in advance. In either case, allow 15 minutes or so for making the dumplings just before serving. The salad can be made early in the day or even the day before. The Pear Crisp is really best made an hour or so before serving and served warm, but it can be made early in the day and warmed in a slow oven.

Serve a dry California Chardonnay with the main course and strong, hot cinnamon-laced coffee with dessert.

Pam's Chicken Fricassee with Wild Mushrooms and Sage

ℰ

SERVES 6 TO 8

¼ cup (½ stick) butter
1 medium onion, thinly sliced
1 garlic clove, crushed
1 celery stalk, thinly sliced
12 ounces button mushrooms, sliced
¼ pound shiitake or other "wild"
   mushrooms, thinly sliced
2 3- to 4-pound fryers, cut up
Salt and finely ground black pepper
3 tablespoons flour
3 cups hot chicken stock
1 cup dry white wine

**A few chickens from my collection
of old farm animal figurines (above).**

**Flowers and comforting foods help chase
away the Sunday night blues (opposite).**

1 teaspoon chopped sage *or* ½ teaspoon
  dried rubbed sage
1 large egg
1 cup milk
2 tablespoons chopped parsley
½ teaspoon lemon juice

1. In a large, deep skillet or large Dutch oven, melt the butter over medium heat. Add the onion, garlic, and celery and sauté 5 minutes. Add the mushrooms and sauté until the vegetables are golden, 3 to 4 minutes longer. Discard the garlic; remove the remaining vegetables with a slotted spoon and reserve.

2. Season the chicken with salt and pepper and sprinkle the flour over it, lightly coating both sides. A few pieces at a time, add the chicken to the pan and sauté until lightly browned, 3 to 5 minutes per side.

3. Add the stock and wine to the pan, raise the heat to high, and bring to a simmer. Reduce the heat to low, cover the pan, and simmer, turning occasionally, until the chicken is cooked through, 25 to 30 minutes. Transfer the chick-

en to a large plate or shallow bowl and keep warm.

4. Add the reserved vegetables and the sage to the pan and raise the heat to medium-high. Cook the liquid, stirring constantly, until it is thickened slightly, about 5 minutes. Remove from the heat and season to taste with salt and pepper.

5. In a medium mixing bowl, whisk together the egg and milk. Very gradually whisk in about 1 cup of the hot mixture, whisking constantly to keep the mixture smooth. Gradually whisk in the remaining hot mixture. Return this sauce mixture to the pan, stir in the parsley and lemon juice. *(Can be made ahead up to this point, cooled, covered, and refrigerated; bring to room temperature before reheating.)*

6. Place the pan over medium-low heat and bring to a low simmer. (Have the dumpling dough ready and add the dumplings at this point—see the recipe below). Arrange the chicken and dumplings on a serving platter and garnish with sprigs of sage and parsley. Pass the sauce separately.

Steamed Parsley Dumplings

❧

SERVES 6

2 cups all-purpose flour
2 teaspoons baking powder
½ teaspoon salt
2 tablespoons butter
¼ cup chopped parsley
¾ cup milk

1. In a mixing bowl, sift together the flour, baking powder, and salt, then cut in the butter. Stir in the parsley, then add the milk and stir with a fork until the dry ingredients are just moistened, forming a soft dough.

2. Using a large spoon, drop the dough onto the simmering fricassee sauce (about 3 tablespoons dough per dumpling), leaving a little space between the dumplings, and cover the pan. Cook 10 minutes before removing the lid (do not lift the lid and peek!). If a cake tester inserted in a dumpling comes out clean, they are done; if not, re-cover the pan and simmer 1 minute longer. Serve immediately.

Note: If all the dumpling dough doesn't fit in the pan at one time, make 1 batch, transfer to a warm plate, and cover loosely to keep warm, then make a second batch.

Cabbage and Carrot Salad with Walnut Dressing

❧

SERVES 4 TO 6

½ head green cabbage, thinly sliced and
  separated into shreds
3 medium carrots, coarsely grated
½ cup coarsely chopped walnuts, lightly
  toasted

Chicken—smothered in a wild mushroom and sage sauce—and dumplings (above left). Crumbly topped Pear-Berry Crisp (left).

Walnut Dressing

¼ cup peanut or vegetable oil

2 tablespoons walnut oil

3 tablespoons cider vinegar

1 teaspoon sugar

1 teaspoon Dijon mustard

¼ teaspoon salt

¼ teaspoon freshly ground black pepper

1 small garlic clove, chopped

1. In a large bowl, combine the cabbage, carrots, and walnuts.

2. In a screwtop jar, combine the oils, vinegar, sugar, mustard, salt, pepper, and garlic. Cover the jar and shake well to blend. Pour the dressing over the vegetable mixture and toss well. Cover and refrigerate for at least 3 hours before serving, tossing once or twice. (*The salad can be made up to 24 hours in advance.*)

Pear-Berry Crisp

SERVES 6

Berries and nuts add color and texture to an old-fashioned favorite. Go ahead and use good store-bought gingersnaps for the crumbs.

THE BEST THINGS ABOUT WINTER

- Oatmeal with bananas for breakfast
- Christmas carols
- Hot soup for supper
- A fire in the fireplace
- Dinner with friends
- An evening snowfall
- Roasting chestnuts
- Candles in the windows
- Tangerines
- Christmas shopping
- Sleeping till long after sunrise
- Looking for Mr. Groundhog

OUTDOOR WINTER VISITORS

Back home, my family always had an open-door policy—if you were driving by, you were welcome to drop in, "set a spell," and have a bite to eat and a chat. I continue that policy today with my friends, neighbors, and my "outdoor family" who live in and around my yard. Feeders hang in the peach tree and on the trellis outside the kitchen window for the feathered friends who join me for breakfast every morning. The family of rabbits who live along the fencerow by the compost heap amuse me with their playing and the squirrels help out with my walnut cleanup every fall, so, in wintertime I return the favor by putting out ears of dried corn. Finally, there are the "black sheep" of my outdoor family, my white-tailed friends, the deer. They *love* my yard and garden—in winter there's almost nothing they won't help themselves to, as long as it's green. Isn't nature wonderful!

---

6 Anjou or Bosc pears, peeled, cored, and sliced

¾ cup raspberries (fresh or frozen)

¼ cup (½ stick) butter, melted

4 tablespoons sugar

½ teaspoon ground cinnamon

1 tablespoon brandy or rum

1 cup coarse gingersnap crumbs

¼ cup sliced almonds

½ pint lowfat yogurt

1. Preheat the oven to 325°F. Lightly butter a 9-inch ceramic or glass pie pan. Arrange the pears snugly in an even layer in the pan and scatter the berries over them. Sprinkle half the sugar over the fruit.

2. In a small bowl, mix the butter, remaining sugar, and cinnamon together, then mix in the brandy, crumbs, and almonds, forming a crumbly mixture. Sprinkle the crumbs over the fruit and bake until the pears are tender, 30 to 40 minutes.

3. Serve warm, with a dollop of yogurt spooned over each serving.

Parlor Game Dinner

FOR 8 TO 10

❧

MENU

Potted Swiss Steak

Mashed Potato Cakes

Winter Succotash

Brussels Sprout and
Broccoli Salad

• • •

Toasted Coconut
Angel Food Squares

Fresh Winter Fruit Compote

When I was in my early teens I spent summers in Indiana at my Grandma and Stepgrandfather Stapleton's horse and sheep farm, helping out while my retired stepgrandfather was away racing his horses at county and state fairs. My grandmother didn't believe in television, so in the evenings after supper we would play all kinds of board games and parlor games. I always thought she was being a little hard on me by not letting me win unless I really beat her (which was very rare), but as I grew older I realized she was only teaching me all about sportsmanship.

I'm still fond of having an evening of games,

from charades to a scavenger hunt, following a casual supper. This is all food that can be prepared in advance and requires very little work or time to get onto the table, and it's all suitable for buffet-style serving.

Getting Ready The Swiss steak and potato cakes can be made completely a day in advance and reheated in the oven before serving. The salad and angel food squares can also be made a day in advance. The succotash can be almost completed the day before, then finished off just before serving (see the recipe). The fruit compote can be prepared a few hours ahead.

Potted Swiss Steak

❧

SERVES 8 TO 10

¼ cup all-purpose flour
½ teaspoon salt
¼ teaspoon freshly ground black pepper
½ teaspoon mild paprika
1 teaspoon dry mustard
3 pounds cubed steak, lightly pounded
and cut into serving-sized pieces
¼ cup vegetable oil
1 garlic clove, chopped
1 medium onion, sliced
1 celery stalk, thinly sliced
1 carrot, thinly sliced
1 14½-ounce can whole tomatoes in
puree, coarsely chopped

1. In a shallow bowl, stir together the flour, salt, pepper, paprika, and dry mustard. Lightly dredge the steak in the flour mixture and set aside. Reserve any leftover flour mixture.

2. In a shallow, nonreactive and flameproof roasting pan or baking dish, heat 2 tablespoons oil over medium heat until sizzling. Add the garlic, onion, carrot, and celery and sauté until golden and tender, 7 to 10 minutes. Remove the vegetables with a slotted spoon and reserve.

A buffet dinner can be served anywhere in the house, even in a book-lined corner.

3. Add the remaining oil to the pan. Lightly brown the steak on both sides. Add the sautéed vegetables and stir in the leftover flour mixture. Add the tomatoes with their puree. Bring the liquid to a boil, then reduce the heat and cover the pan. *(The steak can be made up to a day in advance to this point, covered, and refrigerated; bring to room temperature before proceeding.)*

4. Heat the oven to 350°F. Place the covered pan in the oven and bake until the meat is very tender, 50 to 60 minutes.

Mashed Potato Cakes

❧

SERVES 8 TO 10

Whenever I make mashed potatoes, I always make enough to have some leftovers for potato cakes the next day. In this case it's okay to make the potatoes for the sole purpose of having the cakes, which require no more last-minute preparation than being popped into the oven.

4 pounds boiling potatoes, peeled and quartered
2 tablespoons butter
½ teaspoon salt
¼ teaspoon freshly ground black pepper
½ teaspoon paprika
½ cup milk
1 large egg, lightly beaten
4 scallions, white and green parts, finely chopped
Vegetable oil

1. Place the potatoes in a pot with salted water to cover. Place over medium-high heat and bring to a boil. Boil the potatoes until just tender, about 20 minutes. Drain the potatoes and return them to the pot.

2. Add the butter, salt, pepper, and paprika and mash with a potato masher, leaving a few lumps. In a small bowl or a measuring cup, combine the milk and egg; using a large spoon, beat this mixture into the potatoes until well blended. Add the scallions and mix well.

3. Shape the potato mixture into round thick patties about 3 inches in diameter. Place them on a plate with wax paper between the layers. Wrap well and chill until firm. *(The potato cakes can be made up to a day in advance to this point.)*

4. Preheat the oven to 350°F. Lightly brush the potato cakes on both sides with oil and place them in a single layer on a large baking sheet. Bake until well browned on both sides, 30 to 40 minutes. Serve hot.

Winter Succotash

🙢

SERVES 8

In the summertime I like to cook freshly scraped corn kernels with snap beans, add a dot of butter and a grinding of pepper and that's it. In winter I like this succotash made, from necessity, with frozen vegetables, and it's good.

Even a wintertime meal can be colorful.

1 thin slice bacon, finely chopped
1 small onion, finely chopped
2 10-ounce packages frozen corn kernels, thawed
2 10-ounce packages frozen baby lima beans, thawed
½ cup chicken stock or water
½ cup heavy cream
Salt and coarsely ground black pepper

1. In a Dutch oven over medium heat, sauté the bacon until it begins to brown and render its fat, about 5 minutes. Add the onion and sauté until golden, 5 to 7 minutes longer.

2. Add the corn, lima beans, and chicken stock and bring the mixture to a simmer. Reduce the heat to low, and simmer, stirring occasionally to prevent sticking, until the lima beans are just tender, about 8 minutes. The stock should almost all be evaporated. *(The succotash can be made in advance up to this point and refrigerated.)*

SCAVENGER HUNTS

Scavenger hunts, popular years ago, can still be a lot of fun. Invite everyone to come over early, then divide into teams, set the time limit, and pass out the list (and remind everyone to drive safely). Don't forget to have prizes ready, along with dinner, when everyone comes back. Here's a list of suggestions, but anything goes.

1. Ticket stubs from a certain movie (or play, concert, or sports event)

2. A menu from a particular restaurant

3. A picture of Greta Garbo (or some other noncurrent movie or music star)

4. An autograph from a famous person (not from the entertainment world)

5. A maple leaf (or holly leaf, or acorn, or pine cone)

6. A buffalo head nickel (or a £1 note)

7. The *original* Broadway cast recording of *Guys and Dolls* on LP (or the Beatles' *White Album* or some other classic recording—no tapes or CDs allowed)

8. A Valentine (or Mother's Day or Father's Day card)

9. A chocolate anything (except cookies or candy)

10. A hardcover edition of *Gone With the Wind*

---

3. Stir in the cream, raise the heat to medium, and bring to a simmer. Cook, stirring constantly, until the cream thickens, 3 or 4 minutes. Season to taste with salt and pepper and serve hot.

Brussels Sprout and Broccoli Salad

🙢

SERVES 8 TO 10

2 10-ounce cartons Brussels sprouts
1 large head broccoli, cut into flowerets

Dressing

¼ cup virgin olive oil
½ cup lemon juice
2 large garlic cloves, crushed
2 bay leaves
2 teaspoons chopped tarragon *or* ½
    teaspoon dried tarragon
1 tablespoon chopped parsley
½ teaspoon salt
¼ teaspoon sugar
¼ teaspoon red pepper flakes

1. Remove the outer leaves from the Brussels sprouts, rinse them well, and cut an X into the stem ends. One at a time, place the vegetables in a steamer basket and place over simmering water. Cover and steam until the vegetables are crisp-tender, 7 to 10 minutes. Transfer the vegetables to a large bowl.

2. While the vegetables are cooking, make the dressing: Combine the dressing ingredients in a jar and shake well. Pour the hot dressing over the hot vegetables, toss well, and allow to cool.

3. Cover the bowl tightly and chill overnight, tossing once or twice. Remove from the refrigerator and pick out the garlic cloves about half an hour before serving.

Toasted Coconut Angel Food Squares

MAKES 16 SQUARES

These are a cross between angel food cake and coconut macaroons. And what could be better than that?

9 egg whites
¾ teaspoon cream of tartar
¼ teaspoon salt
¾ cup sugar
¾ cup sifted cake flour
1 teaspoon vanilla extract
½ teaspoon grated lemon rind
1¼ cup sweetened flaked coconut

1. Preheat the oven to 325°F. Have ready an ungreased 9-inch square cake pan.

2. In an impeccably clean bowl, beat the egg whites until very soft peaks begin to form, then beat in the cream of tartar and salt. Gradually beat in the sugar, continuing to beat until stiff and shiny peaks form. Sprinkle the flour over the egg whites and gently fold it in. Fold in the vanilla, lemon rind, and ¾ cup coconut.

3. Using a rubber spatula, spread the batter evenly into the pan and sprinkle the remaining ½ cup coconut over it. Bake until the coconut is golden brown and a toothpick or cake tester inserted in the center comes out clean, about 25 to 30 minutes. Place the pan on a wire rack and cool until just barely warm, cut the cake into squares, then cool completely.

Angel food squares and fresh fruit are a light ending to a hearty dinner.

Fresh Winter Fruit Compote

No formal recipe is needed here. In a large glass bowl or jar, combine 8 cups mixed cubed or sliced fruit (oranges, grapefruits, tangerines, pineapple, bananas, grapes, apples, pears, mangoes) with ½ cup applejack or apricot brandy, ½ cup sugar, the juice of a lemon, and a few cinnamon sticks. Toss well, cover, and refrigerate overnight. Toss again before serving.

A Humble Meat Loaf Supper

FOR 6

ℰ𝒶

MENU

Turkey and Spinach Loaf

Green Pea Puree

Egg Noodles with Mushrooms
and Caraway

Wilted Chicory and Escarole
Salad with Apple

...

Lemon Meringue
Bread-and-Butter Pudding

**After an afternoon "out on the slopes,"
a comforting dinner fits the bill.**

I can't think of anything more down-home than the humble, all-American meat loaf for a casual, satisfying supper. Anyone who cooks at all has a favorite meat loaf recipe—there must be a million ways to make it. My old friend and former neighbor, Rob Miller, is a meat loaf connoisseur, but don't ever ask him how he makes it, because it's different every time (and he's not about to give away any secrets). You just know that if you're invited for dinner, it's bound to be meat loaf, and it's bound to be good.

Getting Ready Meat loaf is easy to make, so just schedule to get it into the oven about an hour and a half before serving. Start the noodles about half an hour before serving time, and the peas and salad dressing about 15 minutes before serving. The salad greens can be readied anytime during the day, then tossed. Dessert can be made anytime during the day.

Turkey and Spinach Loaf

ℰ𝒶

MAKES 2 LOAVES,
SERVING 6 EACH

Once I had the notion of making a meat loaf using ground turkey, it took quite a few tries to get one that tasted like anything at all. So, after much experimentation, here's turkey loaf number 29.

Whenever I make meat loaf it's always one for tonight's dinner and one for the freezer. I never bake meat loaf in a loaf pan, since they tend to "stew in their own juice" that way. This recipe has a simple tomato sauce that cooks in the pan right along with the loaves.

1 cup (1 8-ounce can) tomato sauce
2 pounds ground turkey
1 pound ground lean pork

I don't think twice about serving dinner in the kitchen—even to company.

½ cup freshly grated Parmesan cheese

2 10-ounce packages spinach, thawed and squeezed dry

½ cup finely chopped parsley

1 medium onion, chopped

3 large garlic cloves, chopped

2 large eggs

1 cup fine, dry bread crumbs

¼ teaspoon salt

¾ teaspoon finely ground black pepper

1 teaspoon dried marjoram

1 teaspoon dried thyme

Sauce

1 medium onion, chopped

1 28-ounce can plum tomatoes in puree

1. Preheat the oven to 350°F.

2. In a large bowl, combine all the ingredients and mix well with your hands. Shape the mixture into two loaves and place them in a shallow baking pan large enough to hold the two loaves.

3. For the sauce, combine the onion and tomatoes in the bowl and break up the tomatoes slightly with the back of a large spoon. Pour the mixture over the loaves.

4. Bake the loaves, basting occasionally with the pan juices, until firm and well browned, 1 to 1¼ hours. Remove the pan from the oven and transfer to a cutting board. Cover the loaves loosely with foil and let stand 15 minutes or so before slicing.

Green Pea Puree
SERVES 6

Here's a different way to have peas with meat loaf. Out of season, it's fine to make this with frozen peas.

3 cups fresh peas or frozen peas, thawed

2 tablespoons butter

2 tablespoons milk

⅛ teaspoon dried tarragon

Pinch of grated nutmeg

Salt and finely ground black pepper

In a saucepan with salted water to cover, cook the peas over medium heat until just tender, 7 to 10 minutes for fresh, 3 to 5 minutes for frozen. Drain the peas and transfer them to the bowl of a food processor fitted with the steel chopping blade. Add the butter, milk, tarragon, and nutmeg, then process until smooth. Season to taste with salt and pepper and serve hot.

My version of the blue plate special—a new kind of meat loaf, noodles, and pureed peas.

Egg Noodles with Mushrooms and Caraway

৯৯

SERVES 6

No fancy pasta dish with exotic ingredients here, just old-fashioned country-style noodles.

2 tablespoons butter
1 tablespoon vegetable oil
1 small onion, chopped
1 carrot, thinly sliced
12 ounces button mushrooms, sliced
½ teaspoon mild paprika
½ teaspoon caraway seeds
1 pound wide egg noodles
Salt and coarsely ground black pepper

1. In a skillet over medium heat, combine the butter and vegetable oil and heat to sizzling. Add the onion and carrot, and sauté until crisp-tender, about 10 minutes. Add the mushrooms and sauté until lightly browned, about 7 minutes longer. Stir in the paprika and caraway seeds, sauté 1 minute, and remove from the heat.

2. Meanwhile, in a large pot of salted water, boil the noodles until al dente (timing depends on

the thickness of the noodles). Drain the noodles and return them to the pot. Add the skillet mixture and toss well. Season to taste and serve.

Wilted Chicory and Escarole Salad with Apple

৯৯

SERVES 6

Dressing
4 thin slices bacon, coarsely chopped
1 garlic clove, finely chopped
⅓ cup olive oil
1 teaspoon flour
1 tablespoon sugar
¼ cup cider vinegar

...

1 head chicory, torn into bite-size pieces
1 head escarole, torn into bite-size pieces
1 medium tart apple, peeled, cored, and
   thinly sliced

1. In a small skillet over medium-low heat, sauté the bacon and garlic in the oil until the bacon is lightly browned and crisp. Whisk in the flour, then the sugar and vinegar and continue sautéing until the mixture is slightly thickened.

2. In a serving bowl, toss the greens and apples together, pour the hot dressing over them, and toss again. Serve immediately.

Lemon Meringue Bread-and-Butter Pudding

ℬ

SERVES 6 TO 8

¼ cup (½ stick) butter, softened
10 thin slices stale white bread
2½ cups milk
6 large egg yolks
Juice and grated rind of 3 lemons
½ cup sugar

Meringue

6 large egg whites
½ teaspoon cream of tartar
½ cup sugar
½ teaspoon vanilla

1. Generously butter 5 slices of the white bread, then top with the remaining slices, making sandwiches. Cut the sandwiches diagonally into quarters and arrange them in a single layer in a lightly buttered, shallow 3-quart baking dish, overlapping the edges slightly.

2. In a mixing bowl, beat the milk, egg yolks, lemon juice and rind, and sugar together until well blended. Pour this mixture over the sandwiches and let stand 15 minutes.

3. Preheat the oven to 350°F. Place the baking dish in a larger pan and pour boiling water into the larger pan to come halfway up the sides of the pudding dish. Carefully place in the oven and bake until the tips of the bread are lightly browned, about 45 minutes. Remove from the oven and lower the heat to 300°F.

4. In a spotlessly clean mixing bowl, beat the egg whites until soft peaks form, add the cream of tartar, and continue beating until the peaks stiffen slightly. Gradually beat in the sugar, then beat in the vanilla.

5. Drop the meringue in big spoonfuls onto the pudding, covering it completely and letting the meringue stand in peaks. Bake until the meringue is lightly browned, 10 to 15 minutes. Allow to cool, then remove the pudding from the larger pan and chill before serving.

Lemon Meringue Bread-and-Butter Pudding—a combination of two of my favorites desserts.

"Come on Over for Coffee and Cake"

✤

Walnut Hill Fudge Cake

Great-Aunt Nina's Whiskey Cake

Lemon-Almond Cupcakes

Iva Mae's Sour Cream Apple Cake

Raspberry "Jam" Cake

Cranberry-Pecan Coffee Cake

Brown Sugar Pound Cake

Chocolate-Orange Marble Cake

Banana Cream Bundt Cake

Poppy Seed Coffee Ring

If I Knew You Were Coming, I'd Have Baked a Cake," that song from the fifties, told the story: All you need to make a guest feel special is a home-baked cake. A simple old-fashioned cake can make any gathering, no matter how spur-of-the-moment or how casual, a little bit nicer. When I was growing up, we almost always had a cake in the house, and so did most other folks, too. Mom worked hard on the farm but she always found time to mix up a mayonnaise cake (a rich fudgy chocolate cake) or a banana walnut cake (the recipes appear in *The Holidays* and *Special Occasions*, respectively) to have them ready for after-school snacks, or drop-in company.

So here are a few of my favorite simple cakes, with no fancy fillings or frostings, perfect for snacking—for a morning coffee break with a neighbor, an after-dinner get-together with a few friends, or even all by yourself on a winter afternoon with a cup of hot tea.

Even the simplest cake can be made special. Here, Walnut Hill Fudge Cake (opposite) is served with raspberries and whipped cream.

Sour cream apple cake (above) is an anytime-of-the-day favorite at my house.

Walnut Hill Fudge Cake

MAKES ONE 9 X 5 X 3-INCH
LOAF CAKE

This is one rich cake, with deep chocolate and intense black walnut flavors and a hint of orange and cinnamon. You almost have to have the cake topped with Vanilla Ice Cream (page 58) or whipped cream; try toasting the cake slices first and maybe topping the cream with berries or a spoonful of Hot Fudge Sauce (page 59). If you can't find black walnuts, lightly toasted English walnuts can be substituted, but the flavor won't be as intense.

CAKE AUCTIONS

For years and years, cakes have been considered great prizes. One old American tradition was the cakewalk, a gathering where men would have to dance and strut their stuff to win the cake (and hopefully the affections) of the lady of choice. And of course there are the cake sales held by all kind of organizations to raise money for their projects.

At my grade school in Steuben, Ohio, the PTA held all kinds of fund-raising events, but the favorite for all of us kids was always the cake auction. Each mother had to bake a cake and of course they all tried to outdo one another. The mothers provided their recipes ahead of time. The recipes were mimeographed and stapled together, then the "cookbooks" were sold at the auction as well. On the night of the auction, all the cakes were displayed on tables in the largest of the four classrooms. Then the auction itself would begin, with exuberant bidding, plenty of bickering, and lots of laughs.

Nowadays, I'm afraid, most of the cakes at cake sales start off with the opening of a cake mix box (why don't people realize that it takes only a few minutes to mix up a cake without a mix?), but in those days, no matter whose cake you ended up buying, you could rest assured you were getting a delicious one — from scratch.

Cocoa, for dusting
1 cup (2 sticks) butter, softened
1 cup sugar
4 large eggs
5 ounces (5 squares) semisweet chocolate, melted and cooled
2 teaspoons vanilla extract
1⅔ cups all-purpose flour
¼ teaspoon salt
¼ teaspoon ground cinnamon
1¼ teaspoons baking powder
¼ teaspoon baking soda
1 cup lowfat yogurt
½ teaspoon grated orange rind
⅔ cup coarsely chopped black walnuts (page 102), lightly toasted
Confectioners' sugar, for dusting

1. Preheat the oven to 325°F. Lightly grease a 9 x 5 x 3-inch loaf pan, line the bottom with wax paper, and grease the wax paper. Dust the pan lightly with cocoa.

2. In a mixing bowl, cream the butter and sugar together until light and fluffy, then beat in the eggs one at a time, beating well after each addition. Beat in the chocolate and the vanilla.

3. In a separate bowl, sift together the flour, salt, cinnamon, baking powder, and baking soda. A third at a time, beat the dry mixture into the wet mixture alternately with the yogurt. Stir in the orange rind and the walnuts.

4. Transfer the batter to the prepared pan. Bake until a toothpick or cake tester comes out clean, about 1 hour. Place the cake on a wire rack and cool it in the pan for 15 minutes, then remove it from the pan and place on the rack to cool completely. Lightly dust the top with confectioners' sugar before serving.

Whiskey Cake is studded with raisins and nuts and topped with a dusting of confectioners' sugar (opposite).

Great-Aunt Nina's Whiskey Cake

୫୬

MAKES ONE 10-INCH TUBE CAKE

Whiskey never passed my Great-Aunt Nina's lips, but she always kept a bottle stashed away on the top shelf of her pantry just for making this cake.

½ cup (1 stick) butter, softened
1¼ cups firmly packed dark brown sugar
3 large eggs
¼ cup Scotch or bourbon whiskey
1 teaspoon vanilla extract
1 cup all-purpose flour
½ teaspoon baking powder
¼ teaspoon baking soda
¼ teaspoon salt
½ teaspoon ground cinnamon
¼ teaspoon ground ginger
¼ teaspoon grated nutmeg
1 teaspoon grated orange rind
2 cups raisins
2 cups chopped walnuts or pecans, lightly toasted
Confectioners' sugar, for dusting

1. Preheat the oven to 350°F. Lightly grease a 10-inch tube pan with a removable bottom.

2. In a mixing bowl, cream the butter and sugar together until light and fluffy. One at a time, beat in the eggs, beating well after each addition, then beat in the whiskey and the vanilla.

3. In a separate bowl, sift together the flour, baking powder, baking soda, salt, and spices. Gradually beat the dry mixture into the wet mixture, then stir in the orange rind, raisins, and nuts.

4. Transfer the batter to the prepared pan. Bake until a toothpick or cake tester comes out clean, 30 to 35 minutes. Place the cake on a wire rack and cool it in the pan for 15 minutes, then remove the outside of the pan. Cool completely before removing the bottom of the pan.

5. Lay a wire rack over the cake and dust lightly with confectioners' sugar before serving.

Lemon – Almond Cupcakes

❧

MAKES 1 DOZEN

⅓ cup (⅔ stick) butter, softened
½ cup sugar
1 large egg
½ teaspoon vanilla extract
Grated rind of 1 lemon
1 cup all-purpose flour
2 teaspoons baking powder
¼ teaspoon salt
¼ cup milk
½ cup sliced almonds
½ cup sugar
Juice of 1 lemon

Cupcakes are always a welcome little treat.

1. Preheat the oven to 350°F. Line a 12-cup muffin pan with fluted paper muffin cups.

2. In a mixing bowl, cream the butter and sugar together until light and fluffy, then beat in the egg, vanilla, and lemon rind. In a separate bowl, sift together the flour, baking powder, and salt. A third at a time, beat the dry mixture into the wet mixture, alternating with the milk.

3. Divide the batter among the muffin cups and sprinkle the almonds over the batter. Bake until the cupcakes are nicely browned and a toothpick or cake tester inserted in the center comes out clean, 20 to 25 minutes.

4. Transfer the cupcakes to wire racks. Stir the sugar and lemon juice together. Brush the mixture over the cupcakes and cool completely.

Iva Mae's Sour Cream Apple Cake

❧

MAKES ONE 10-INCH TUBE CAKE

Apple cakes are the most popular fresh fruit cakes around, and there are probably just as many different kinds as there are apples. This one, with sour cream in batter and apples and cinnamon in the middle and on top, is a favorite in my house.

½ cup (1 stick) butter
1 cup sugar
2 large eggs
1 teaspoon vanilla extract
2 cups all-purpose flour
1 teaspoon baking powder
1 teaspoon baking soda
½ teaspoon salt
1 cup sour cream

Filling/Topping
½ cup sugar
2 teaspoons ground cinnamon
½ cup sugar
½ cup chopped walnuts
2 to 3 apples, peeled, cored, and sliced

1. Preheat the oven to 375°F. Lightly grease a 10-inch round (or heart-shaped) tube pan with a removable bottom.

2. In a mixing bowl, cream together the butter and sugar, then beat in the eggs and vanilla. In a separate bowl sift together the flour, baking powder, baking soda, and salt. A third at a time, beat the dry mixture into the wet mixture, alternately with the sour cream.

3. For the filling/topping, stir the sugar and cinnamon together then stir in the walnuts. Spread half the batter into the prepared pan, top with an overlapping layer of apple slices, then sprinkle half the cinnamon/nut mixture over it. Repeat with the remaining ingredients.

4. Bake until the cake is nicely browned and a cake tester or toothpick inserted in the center comes out clean, about 35 minutes. Remove the pan to a wire rack, cool 30 minutes and remove the outside of the pan. Allow to cool completely before carefully removing the bottom of the pan.

Raspberry "Jam" Cake

MAKES ONE 10-INCH TUBE CAKE

I love the idea of old-fashioned jam cakes, but they always seem a little too sweet. I now use store-bought sugarless fruit spread, which lets the fruit flavor shine through.

¼ cup (½ stick) butter, softened
1 cup sugar
1 large egg
1 cup raspberry fruit spread
1 teaspoon vanilla extract
2 cups all-purpose flour
1 teaspoon baking powder
1 teaspoon baking soda
½ teaspoon salt
½ teaspoon cinnamon
1 cup buttermilk
Confectioners' sugar, for dusting

1. Preheat the oven to 350°F. Lightly grease a 10-inch tube pan (I used a heart-shaped one here).

2. In a mixing bowl, cream the butter and sugar together. Beat in the egg, then beat in the fruit spread and the vanilla. In a separate bowl, sift together the flour, baking powder, soda, salt, and cinnamon. A third at a time, beat the dry mixture into the wet mixture, alternating with the buttermilk.

3. Transfer the batter to the prepared pan and bake until the cake is nicely browned and a cake tester inserted in the center comes out clean, about 45 minutes. Remove the pan to a wire rack and cool 15 minutes, then turn the cake out onto the rack to cool completely.

4. Lay a paper doily or a wire rack over the cake and dust lightly with confectioners' sugar before serving.

I bake a Raspberry "Jam" Cake whenever I have a wintertime craving for berries.

Cranberry–Pecan Coffee Cake

MAKES ONE 9-INCH SQUARE CAKE

A quick cake for during the holidays, when someone's bound to drop by unexpectedly.

¼ cup vegetable shortening
¾ cup sugar
1 large egg
½ teaspoon vanilla
1½ cups all-purpose flour
1 tablespoon baking powder
¼ teaspoon salt
¼ teaspoon ground cloves
½ cup milk
1 cup cranberries
1 teaspoon grated orange rind

Topping
1 cup firmly packed light brown sugar
3 teaspoons ground cinnamon
¼ cup all-purpose flour
¼ cup (½ stick) butter, melted
1 cup coarsely chopped pecans

1. Preheat the oven to 350°F. Lightly grease a 9-inch square cake pan.

2. In a mixing bowl, cream the shortening and sugar together. Beat in the egg, then beat in the vanilla. In a separate bowl, sift together the flour, baking powder, salt, and cloves. A third at a time, beat the dry mixture into the wet mixture, alternating with the milk. Stir in ¾ cup cranberries and the orange rind.

3. To make the topping, combine all the ingredients in a bowl and mix until coarse crumbs are formed.

4. Spread half the batter evenly in the prepared pan, then sprinkle half the topping over it. Repeat with the remaining batter and topping, then scatter the remaining ¼ cup cranberries over all.

5. Bake until a toothpick or cake tester comes out clean, 25 to 30 minutes. Cool in the pan on a wire rack. Serve warm or at room temperature, cut into squares.

Brown Sugar Pound Cake

MAKES ONE 10-INCH TUBE CAKE OR TWO 9 X 5 X 3-INCH LOAF CAKES

Sweet potatoes add moistness and richness replacing some of the butter in this lightly spiced pound cake. The cake freezes well.

½ cup (1 stick) butter, softened
2 cups firmly packed light brown sugar
4 large eggs
1½ teaspoons vanilla extract
2½ cups mashed cooked sweet potatoes
3 cups all-purpose flour
2 teaspoons baking powder
1 teaspoon baking soda
¼ teaspoon salt
1 teaspoon ground ginger
1 teaspoon ground cinnamon
¼ teaspoon grated nutmeg

1. Preheat the oven to 325°F. Lightly grease a 10-inch tube pan or two 9 x 5 x 3-inch loaf pans.

2. In a mixing bowl, cream together the butter and sugar. One at a time, beat in the eggs, beating well after each addition, then beat in the vanilla. Beat in the sweet potatoes. In a separate bowl, sift together the flour, baking powder, baking soda, salt, and spices. A third at a time, beat the dry mixture into the wet mixture until well blended.

3. Transfer the batter to the prepared pan(s) and bake until a toothpick or cake tester comes out clean, about 1 hour for the tube cake or 45 minutes for the loaf cakes. Cool the cakes in the pan for 10 minutes, then remove from the pan(s) and place on a wire rack to cool completely.

Glazed Brown Sugar Pound Cake To glaze, combine 1 cup light brown sugar, 3 tablespoons milk, and 2 tablespoons butter in a small, heavy sauceapan. Over medium heat, bring the mixture to a boil, stirring constantly. Remove from the heat and stir in ½ cup sifted confectioners' sugar and then ½ teaspoon vanilla. Drizzle the warm glaze over the cake.

Chocolate–Orange Marble Cake

MAKES ONE 10-INCH TUBE CAKE

A bit of orange zest and a touch of cinnamon add just a little zip to this old-fashioned favorite without changing its no-nonsense character.

⅓ cup vegetable shortening
1 cup sugar
2 large eggs
1 teaspoon vanilla
1¾ cups cake flour
2 teaspoons baking powder
½ teaspoon salt
½ cup milk
1 ounce semisweet chocolate, melted
1 teaspoon ground cinnamon
1 teaspoon grated orange rind

1. Preheat the oven to 350°F. Lightly grease a 10-inch tube pan.

2. In a mixing bowl, cream together the shortening and sugar until light and fluffy. Beat in the eggs, then the vanilla. In a separate bowl, sift the dry ingredients together. A third at a time, beat the dry mixture into the wet mixture, alternating with the milk. Transfer half the batter to a separate bowl.

3. Beat the chocolate and cinnamon into one portion of the batter and stir the orange rind into the other portion. Alternately drop large spoonfuls of the batter into the prepared pan. When all the batter is in the pan, insert a knife in the batter and run it once around the pan to swirl the batters together slightly.

4. Bake until the cake is nicely browned and a toothpick or cake tester comes out clean, 50 to 60 minutes. Place the pan on a wire rack and allow the cake to cool 5 minutes, then remove the cake from the pan and place on the rack to cool completely.

Chocolate–Orange Marble Cake, glazed Brown Sugar Poundcake, and Cranberry–Pecan Coffee Cake (top to bottom).

Banana Cream Bundt Cake

MAKES ONE 10-INCH BUNDT CAKE

½ cup vegetable shortening
1½ cups sugar
2 large eggs
3 cups all-purpose flour
1 teaspoon baking powder
1 teaspoon baking soda
½ teaspoon salt
1 teaspoon ground cinnamon
½ teaspoon ground cardamom
½ teaspoon grated nutmeg
⅓ cup lemon juice
1 teaspoon vanilla extract
3 very ripe bananas, mashed
1 cup chopped walnuts

Filling

2 3-ounce packages cream cheese, softened
¼ cup sugar
½ teaspoon ground cinnamon
¼ teaspoon salt
1 large egg
1 tablespoon all-purpose flour
1 teaspoon vanilla extract

▪▪▪

2 tablespoons butter, melted
2 tablespoons sugar

A few roses decorate a simple banana cake.

1. In a mixing bowl, cream together the shortening and 1½ cups sugar, then beat in the eggs one at a time, beating well after each addition. In a separate bowl, sift together the flour, baking powder, baking soda, salt, and spices. A third at a time, beat the dry mixture into the wet mixture, alternating with the lemon juice. Beat in the vanilla and bananas, then stir in the nuts.

2. Make the filling by combining all the ingredients and beating to blend well. Spread half the batter into the prepared pan, drop the filling over the batter, then top with the remaining batter.

3. Bake until the edges are nicely browned and come away from the sides of the pan, about 50 minutes. Cool the cake in the pan for 15 minutes, then invert onto a wire rack. Brush the cake with the 2 tablespoons melted butter, sprinkle lightly with the 2 tablespoons sugar, then allow to cool completely.

Poppy Seed Coffee Ring

MAKES ONE 9-INCH RING CAKE

Everyone should have one yeast coffee cake up his sleeve, and this is my standby, with a poppy seed filling and an orange glaze.

1 package active dry yeast
¼ cup lukewarm water
¼ cup milk, at room temperature
½ cup (1 stick) butter, softened
¼ cup sugar
2 large eggs
¼ teaspoon salt
2 tablespoons orange juice
1 tablespoon grated orange rind
3 cups all-purpose flour

This coffee ring reminds me of my Great Aunt Susie, who was famous for her coffee cakes.

Filling

1 cup (4 ounces) poppy seeds
1 medium tart apple, peeled, cored, and
    coarsely chopped
2 tablespoons light brown sugar
2 tablespoons flour
2 tablespoons orange juice
¼ teaspoon salt

Glaze

½ cup confectioners' sugar
2 tablespoons orange juice

1. In a small bowl, combine the yeast and water to soften the yeast, then stir in the milk. Set aside.

2. In a large mixing bowl, cream the butter and sugar together until light and fluffy. Beat in the eggs, then the salt, orange juice, and rind. A third at a time, beat the flour into this mixture alternately with the yeast mixture.

3. Transfer the dough to a lightly floured work surface. Knead the dough until smooth and satiny, then form it into a ball. Place in a lightly oiled bowl, cover with a clean cloth, and allow to double in bulk, 1 to 1½ hours.

4. In the bowl of a food processor fitted with the steel chopping blade, combine the filling ingredients. Pulse-process until the ingredients are mixed well and the apple is finely chopped. Set aside.

5. Punch down the dough, then roll it into a rectangle about 16 x 20 inches. Spread the filling mixture evenly over the dough, leaving a ½-inch edge uncovered. With the short side facing you, Carefully roll the dough up like a jelly roll, then pull the 2 ends together, moisten the ends with water, and seal, forming a ring, sealed side down.

6. From the outer edge, cut slashes about 1½ inches apart not quite all the way through the ring, leaving the dough attached at the center. Place the ring in a lightly oiled 9-inch cake pan. Cover the pan with the cloth, then allow to rise until doubled in bulk, 45 minutes to an hour.

7. Preheat the oven to 350°F. Place the pan in the oven and bake until the cake is nicely browned and sounds hollow when tapped with a finger, 30 to 35 minutes. Transfer the cake to a wire rack to cool. To make the glaze, stir the confectioners' sugar and orange juice together with a fork until smooth. Drizzle the glaze over the cake while it's still slightly warm.

Almond Coffee Ring Substitute 1½ cups almond paste mixed with ½ cup raisins for the filling. After glazing the cake, sprinkle with toasted sliced almonds.

Index

૪ઝ

CONVERSION CHART
Equivalent Imperial and Metric Measurements

American cooks use standard containers, the 8-ounce cup and a tablespoon that takes exactly 16 level fillings to fill that cup level. Measuring by cup makes it very difficult to give weight equivalents, as a cup of densely packed butter will weigh considerably more than a cup of flour. The easiest way therefore to deal with cup measurements in recipes is to take the amount by volume rather than by weight. Thus the equation reads:

1 cup = 240 ml = 8 fl. oz.   ½ cup = 120 ml = 4 fl. oz.

It is possible to buy a set of American cup measures in major stores around the world.

In the States, butter is often measured in sticks. One stick is the equivalent of 8 tablespoons. One tablespoon of butter is therefore the equivalent to ½ ounce /15 grams.

Liquid Measures

Fluid ounces	U.S.	Imperial	Milliliters
	1 teaspoon	1 teaspoon	5
¼	2 teaspoon	1 dessert spoon	7
½	1 tablespoon	1 tablespoon	15
1	2 tablespoon	2 tablespoon	28
2	¼ cup	4 tablespoon	56
4	½ cup or ¼ pint		110
5		¼ pint or 1 gill	140
6	¾ cup		170
8	1 cup or ½ pint		225
9			250, ¼ liter
10	1¼ cups	½ pint	280
12	1½ cups	¾ pint	340
15		¾ pint	420
16	2 cups or 1 pint		450
18	2¼ cups		500, ½ liter
20	2½ cups	1 pint	560
24	3 cups or 1½ pints		675
25		1¼ pints	700
27	3½ cups		750
30	3¾ cups	1½ pints	840
32	4 cups or 2 pints or 1 quart	900	
35		1¾ pints	980
36	4 ½ cups		1000, 1 liter
40	5 cups or 2½ pints	2 pints or 1 quart	1120
48	6 cups or 3 pints		1350
50		2½ pints	1400
60	7½ cups	3 pints	1680
64	8 cups or 4 pints or 2 quarts		1800
72	9 cups		2000, 2 liters

Solid Measures

U.S. and Imperial Measures		Metric Measures	
OUNCES	POUNDS	GRAMS	KILOS
1		28	
2		56	
3	½	100	
4	¼	112	
5		140	
6		168	
8	½	225	
9		250	¼
12	¾	340	
16	1	450	
18		500	½
20	1¼	560	
24	1½	675	
27		750	¾
28	1¾	780	
32	2	900	
36	2¼	1000	1
40	2½	1100	
48	3	1350	
54		1500	1½
64	4	1800	
72	4½	2000	2
80	5	2250	2¼
90		2500	2½
100	6	2800	2¾

Oven Temperature Equivalents

Fahrenheit	Celsius	Gas Mark	Description
225	110	¼	Cool
250	130	½	
275	140	1	Very Slow
300	150	2	
325	170	3	Slow
350	180	4	Moderate
375	190	5	
400	200	6	Moderately Hot
425	220	7	Fairly Hot
450	230	8	Hot
475	240	9	Very Hot
500	250	10	Extremely Hot

Linear and Area Measures

1 inch	2.54 centimeters
1 foot	0.3048 meters
1 square inch	6.4516 square centimeters
1 square foot	929.03 square centimeters